LabSim®

The Lessons Only Experience Can Teach

Installation Instructions

Internet Access:
This product requires a connection to the Internet.

Installing and Using LabSim

Installation:
1. Insert the LabSim DVD and click **Launch LabSim**.
2. If the autorun screen does not appear, launch autorun.exe from your DVD drive.
3. Click **Next** at the Welcome screen.
4. Read the license agreement, click **I accept**, then click **Next**
5. View the read me file and click **Next**.
6. Select a destination directory and click **Next**.
7. At the Ready to Install screen, click **Install**.
8. Click **Finish**.
9. Use the **LabSim** shortcut on the desktop, or click
   Windows Start Button > All Programs > LabSim.
10. If you already have an account, enter the login and password.
11. If you have an activation code but you do not have a LabSim account, create an account by clicking the **Create an Account** button and entering the required information. If you do not have a LabSim account and you did not receive an activation code, check with your school, company, or TestOut account representative to see if an account has already been created for you.
12. If you have additional activation codes, click the **Add a LabSim** button from the LabSim Home page.
13. Enter the activation code and click **Activate** to add additional titles to the library.

Launching and Navigating LabSim Titles:
The LabSim Home page displays the list of titles that have been activated for your account. To launch a course, click the course's title.

Installing LabSim Titles to Hard Drive:
You may optionally install LabSim content to your hard drive to eliminate the need to insert the DVD when you launch a title. To install content to your hard drive:
1. After launching a LabSim title, click the **Copy to Hard Drive** button at the bottom of the navigation panel.
2. Select the location for the LabSim content.
3. Wait for the content to be copied to your hard drive.
4. After the content has been copied to your hard drive, you have the option to check for updated content for the LabSim title. Click Yes to allow LabSim to check for updated content.

Checking for LabSim Updates:
You can check for updates for LabSim titles at any time from the Install / Uninstall page by clicking **Check for LabSim Patches**. This feature will check for updated content for the selected content source.

LabSim®

A+ IT Technician

Trademarks

TestOut is a registered trademark of TestOut Corporation.
Cisco Systems is a trademark of Cisco Systems, Inc.
Novell is a registered trademark of Novell, Inc.
NetWare is a registered trademark of Novell, Inc.
Novell Directory Services is a registered trademark of Novell, Inc.
CNA is either a registered trademark or trademark of Novell, Inc.
IPX is a trademark of Novell, Inc.
IPX/SPX is a trademark of Novell, Inc.
Microsoft is either a registered trademark or trademark of Microsoft Corporation in the United States and/or other countries.
Windows is either a registered trademark or trademark of Microsoft Corporation in the United States and/or other countries.
Windows NT is either a registered trademark or trademark of Microsoft Corporation in the United States and/or other countries.
MCAD is either a registered trademark or trademark of Microsoft Corporation in the United States and/or other countries.
MCSE is either a registered trademark or trademark of Microsoft Corporation in the United States and/or other countries.
MCSA is either a registered trademark or trademark of Microsoft Corporation in the United States and/or other countries.
MCP is either a registered trademark or trademark of Microsoft Corporation in the United States and/or other countries.
CCNA is either a registered trademark or trademark of Cisco Systems, Inc.
A+ is either a registered trademark or trademark of CompTIA, Inc.
Linux+ is either a registered trademark or trademark of CompTIA, Inc.
Network+ is either a registered trademark or trademark of CompTIA, Inc.
Security+ is either a registered trademark or trademark of CompTIA, Inc.
UNIX is a registered trademark, licensed exclusively through X/Open Company, Ltd.
All other brand and product names, fonts and company names and logos are trademarks or registered trademarks of their respective companies.

Contents

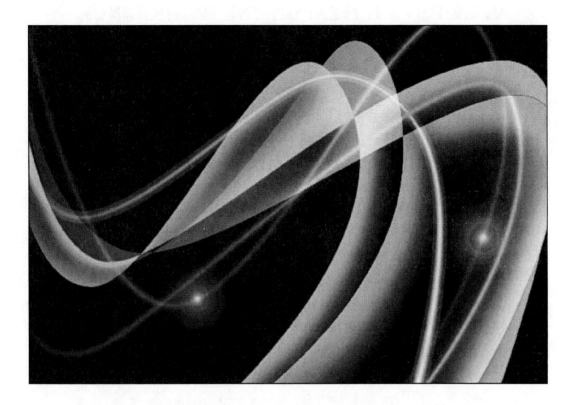

0.0
Introduction

0.4.2 PUT AN ITEM ON THE WORKBENCH

Scenario

Welcome to the TestOut Hardware Simulator. To begin, notice that your screen is divided into three major areas:

- **Scenario** (upper right). The Scenario window gives you information about what you need to do (you are currently reading text in the Scenario window).

- **Shelf** (left side of the screen). The Shelf window lists hardware items that are available for you to install.

- **Workbench** (bottom right). The Workbench window shows all hardware items that are currently installed.

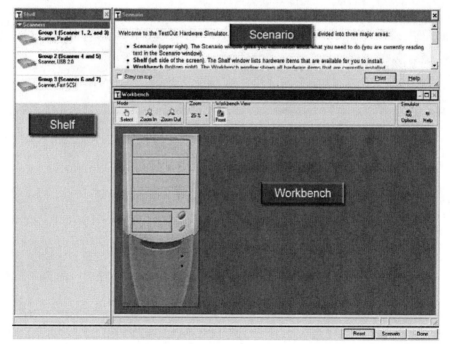

To practice using the TestOut Hardware Simulator, complete the following task:

- From the shelf, select the USB scanner.

- Place the scanner next to the computer on the workbench.

Click the **Done** button at the bottom of the screen when you are finished.

Steps

Complete the following steps:

1. In the Shelf, locate the scanner required by the scenario.

2. Click and hold any part of the scanner. Drag the mouse to the empty space on either side of the computer case in the Workbench.

3.   Release the mouse when you see a white bar with arrows that indicates that the item will be inserted on the Workbench.

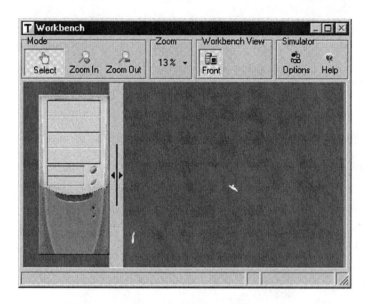

0.4.3 SELECT AN ITEM BASED ON ITS DOCUMENTATION

Scenario

In this lab, you will learn how to get details about a hardware item on the Shelf or Workbench. Two types of details are:

- **Views.** Multiple views of a hardware item are usually available. These views are normally much bigger than the item's icon shown on the Shelf.

- **Documentation.** Some hardware items have documentation that goes beyond the item's description.

To learn how to view and use item details, complete the following task:

1. For each item in the Shelf, click the Details link to view pictures and documentation for the device.

2. Find the device that includes an optional printer port.

3. Add that device to the Workbench next to the computer.

Click the **Done** button at the bottom of the screen when you are finished.

Steps

In this lab, you will need to read the documentation to find the correct component to install.

Complete the following steps:

1. To view the documentation for a scanner, click the **Details** link for a scanner in the Shelf.

2. Click the **Documentation** tab. An overview of the scanner's ports and controls similar to this one is shown.

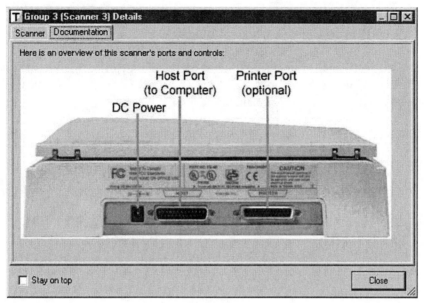

3. Review the documentation for the scanner, then complete the following table with the necessary values.

Scanner	Power Type	Number of Ports	Types of Ports
Ex.: Scanner 1	DC Power	2	High Density 50 Pin SCSI

4. Repeat steps 1 through 3 for each scanner.

5. Based on the information in the table, select the scanner required by the scenario and drag it to the Workbench.

0.4.4 SELECT ITEM CATEGORIES

Scenario

In this lab, you will learn about categories of items on the shelf. Notice that the shelf has two categories of items: Printers and Scanners. Click each category to see the available items. Notice that categories are listed on the shelf alphabetically.

Practice selecting objects by completing the following tasks:

- Place a scanner on the Workbench.

- Place a printer on the Workbench.

Click the **Done** button at the bottom of the screen when you are finished.

Steps

Complete the following steps:

1. Verify that the Scanners category is open, then select a scanner and drag it to the Workbench.

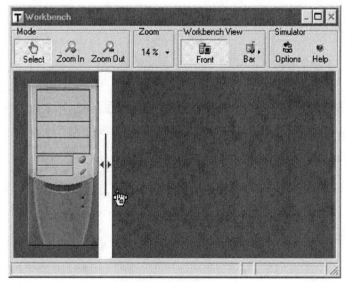

2. Select the **Printers** category.

   Which printer has a 16 page per minute (PPM) output?

   _____

   Which Inkjet printer has a higher PPM? Why?

   _____

3. Select a printer and drag it to the Workbench.

0.4.6 SET DIALS AND SWITCHES

Scenario

Some hardware items have action areas (controls such as dials, buttons, or switches). You can manipulate action areas by clicking or shift-clicking them. To learn how to use action areas, complete the following tasks:

- Switch to the Back view to see the back of the external CD drive.

- Zoom in on the view until you can clearly see the controls on the drive.

- Set the round dial on this CD drive to 4.

- Put the TERM switch in the ON position (the switch should be pointing to the right).

Click the **Done** button at the bottom of the screen when you are finished.

Steps

Complete the following steps:

1. To set the SCSI ID for the CD drive, change to the Back Workbench view.

2. On the Workbench toolbar, click the **Zoom In** button, then click the **SCSI ID** dial (the blue dial) on the back of the CD drive until it is big enough to work with as shown in the graphic below.

3. On the Workbench toolbar, click the **Select** button.

4. With the SCSI ID dial magnified, you can set it to the correct position. To set the dial to the correct position, click (or press the Shift key and click) the arrow in the center of the blue dial to turn it. Continue clicking the arrow until it points to the appropriate setting. (**Note:** You can also click a specific number to set the dial to that number directly.)

5. With the SCSI ID configured, you need to set the TERM switch to ON. To do this, locate the set of small, white configuration switches below the SCSI ID dial. To set the TERM switch to ON, click the second configuration switch. The switch moves to the right, which is the ON position.

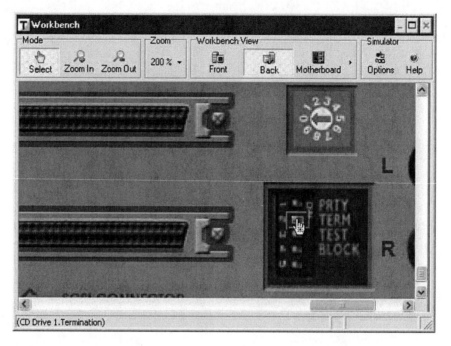

0.4.9 ADD CABLED COMPONENTS

Scenario

Many hardware devices are connected to the computer, or to each other, using cables. In this lab, you will learn how to install cabled devices. Cables or items connected with a cable will appear in the following area:

- **Workbench Connections.** The right side of the Workbench shows all cables or devices that include cables. Read the descriptions for each object to identify where the cable is connected.

To learn how to work with cabled devices, complete the following tasks:

- Put a mouse on the Workbench.

- Connect the mouse to the computer's mouse port (be sure to switch to the Back view of the computer).

- In the Drive Bays Workbench view, put a second hard drive in this computer above the existing hard drive.

- Open the Cables category on the Shelf and attach Connector 1 of the cable on the Shelf to the *existing* hard drive.

- Attach Connector 2 of the cable to the *second hard drive* you just installed.

- Attach Connector 3 of the cable to the motherboard (you will need to switch to Motherboard view).

Click the **Done** button at the bottom of the screen, when you are finished.

Steps

Complete the following steps:

1. To install a mouse, in the Shelf, select the **Mice** category.

2. Drag the mouse (not its connector) and drop it in the empty Workbench space next to the computer. The connector moves to Workbench Connections. Your screen should look similar to this graphic.

3. Change to Back Workbench view.

4. In Workbench Connections, you can select and drag connectors for unconnected devices to their appropriate connectors on the computer. To connect the mouse to the computer, drag the mouse connector from the Workbench Connections to the bright green round mouse port on the back of the computer, shown in this graphic.

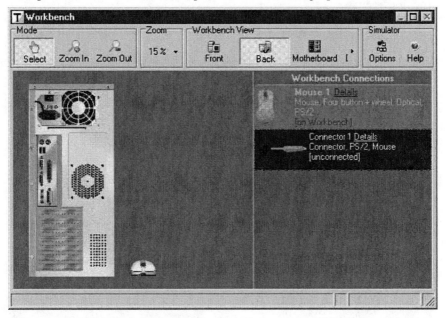

5. To install a second hard drive, change to the Drive Bays Workbench view.

6. Select the **Hard Drive** category on the Shelf.

7. Drag the hard drive to the drive bay above the existing hard drive and drop it when the drive bay highlights.

8. To connect the hard drive cables to the motherboard, in the Shelf, select the **Cables** category.

9. Drag **Connector 1** from the Shelf to the IDE port on the back of the existing hard drive. Make sure the port is highlighted with a blue outline as shown in this graphic before you release the mouse. (If you need help identifying the hard drive's IDE port, read the hard drive's documentation prior to performing this step. The IDE port is labeled "IDE Pin 1" in the documentation.)

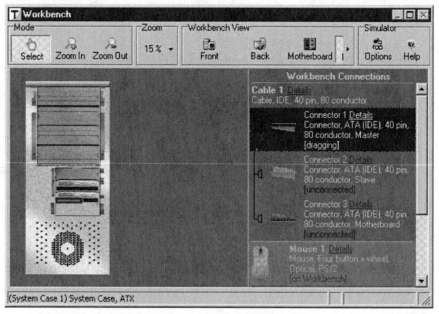

10. Drag **Connector 2** from the Shelf to the IDE port on the back of the second hard drive you just installed. Make sure the port is highlighted before you release the mouse.

11. Change to the Motherboard view.

12. Drag **Connector 3** from the Workbench Connections list to an IDE port on the motherboard. Make sure the port is highlighted, as shown in this graphic, before you release the mouse.

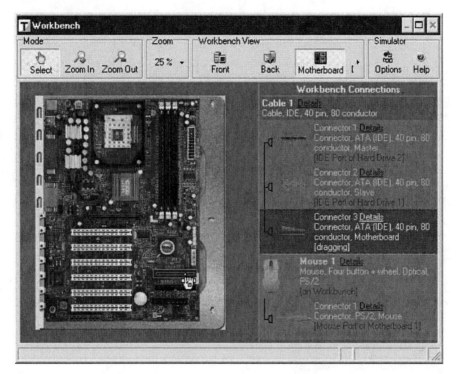

0.4.10 USING THE XP SIMULATOR

Scenario

In this lab, you will learn about key features of the Windows XP simulator. Complete the following steps:

1. Click the **Start** button (lower left hand side of the screen), then click **My Computer**. A graphic similar to this one is shown.

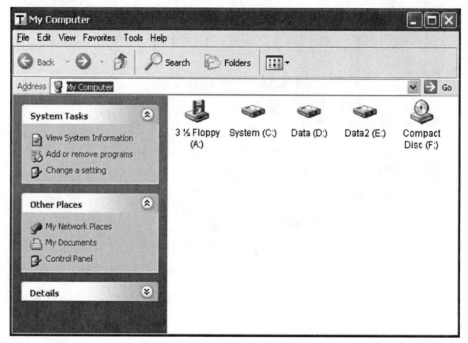

You are now looking at the file system of a simulated computer. The drives that you see in My Computer exist only within the lab, not on your real computer.

2. Double-click the **A:** drive to view the simulated contents of the drive. The following window is shown.

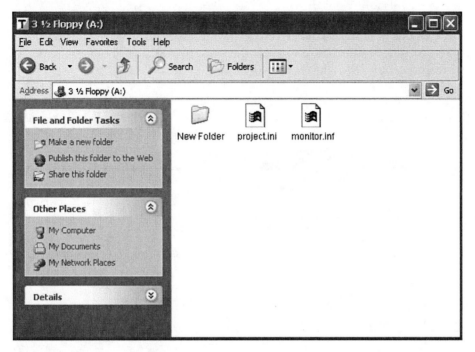

3. Right-click the **Project.ini** file and select **Delete....** This will delete the simulated file, but will not affect files on your real computer.

4. Click **Yes** to confirm the delete.

5. If you make a mistake in the lab, you can reset it without exiting the simulated desktop. Click the **Reset** button (lower right hand side of your screen) to reset the lab.

6. Click **Start, My Computer,** then double-click the **A:** drive again.

   Notice that the file you deleted earlier has been restored.

7. Now select the **New Folder** folder, then click the **Rename this folder** link on the left side of the window. Type **Documents** for the new name.

8. Although many of the features of Windows XP have been simulated, not every feature is important to completing a lab. For example, with the Documents folder selected, click the **Move this folder** link.

    Because this feature has not been enabled within the lab, nothing happens. If you want to do a task but the way that you have chosen doesn't work, try another method (such as a different menu or by right-clicking an object).

9. When you are finished completing all tasks, click the **Done** button on the lower right corner of the screen. You will then be scored on the tasks that you should have completed within the lab, as you see in the graphic shown here.

10. On the score report screen, click the **Explanation** button for help with the steps required to complete all tasks successfully.

    The Explanation portion of the lab gives you additional information about how you should have completed the lab. To get the most out of the learning experience, you should try to complete the lab on your own before you look at the detailed instructions in the Explanation.

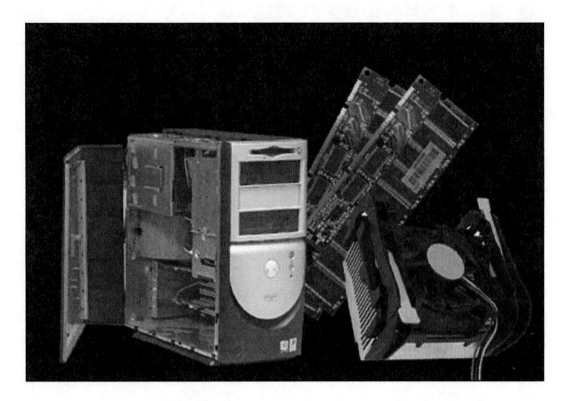

2.0
System Components

2.1.4 FIND BIOS SETTINGS

Enter the CMOS setup program and use the interface to find the following information:

- What is the system memory speed?

- How much L2 cache does the processor have?

- Which IRQ is currently available (not reserved)?

- What is the floppy diskette size?

- Is power management enabled or disabled?

- What is the first boot device?

Note: If you need to restart the simulated computer during the lab, use the Power On/Power Off button in the lower left corner of the interface.

Explanation

Click the **Lab** button and press F1 to enter the CMOS setup program to find the information to complete the following table. One way to find settings is to select various menus and examine the options. Use the information you find to answer the questions in the scenario.

Parameter	Screen Name	Value
System Memory Speed		
L2 Cache RAM Amount		
Available IRQ		
Floppy Diskette Size		
Power Management		
First Boot Device		

2.1.5 TURN ON NUM LOCK

Scenario

A user frequently uses the keyboard's number pad to type numbers in a software program. However, every time the user boots the computer, the NumLock function is Off. The user asks you how to configure the computer so that the NumLock function will be On each time the computer starts. Configure the computer appropriately. Remember to save your changes.

Note: If you need to restart the simulated computer during the lab, use the Power On/Power Off button in the lower left corner of the interface.

Steps

To make changes to different system components through the BIOS, navigate the menus at the tops of the screen. Each menu allows you to access specific components. Also within each menu, you'll find sub menus that allow you to make several changes for a specific device type, such as hard drives, keyboards, peripherals, or displays.

Complete the following steps:

1. To enter the CMOS setup, press F1.

2. Press the Right arrow key to select the **Advanced** menu.

3. Use the Down arrow key to select the **Keyboard Configuration** sub menu. Press Enter.

    What options can you set in this menu?

    _____

4. Make sure that **Numlock** is highlighted and press Enter.

5. Use the Up arrow to highlight **On**, then press Enter.

6. Press F10 to save the changes and press Enter to exit the BIOS.

2.1.6 DISABLE ONBOARD DEVICES

Scenario

You are in the process of configuring a new computer. The motherboard has several built-in devices, but you want to install expansion cards instead to take advantage of components with greater capabilities than the onboard devices.

Your task in this lab is to disable the following onboard devices:

- Video card

- Sound device

- Network adapter

Steps

To make changes to different system components through the BIOS, navigate the menus at the tops of the screen. Each menu allows you to access specific components. Also within each menu, you'll find sub menus that allow you to make several changes for a specific device type, such as hard drives, keyboards, peripherals, or displays.

Complete the following steps:

1. To enter the CMOS setup, press F1.

2. Press the Right arrow key to select the **Advanced** menu. The following screen is shown.

3. Use the Down arrow key to select the **Peripheral Configuration** sub menu, then press Enter. The following screen is shown.

```
PhoenixBIOS Simulator                                          _ □ ×
                              BIOS SETUP UTILITY
        Advanced

  Peripheral Configuration                    Configure serial port A

  Serial Port A  [Disabled]                   Setting this field to
  Serial Port B  [Disabled]                   Auto will enable this
  Parallel Port  [Disabled]                   device, but the BIOS
                                              will not place its
  Onboard Audio  [Enabled]                    resources unless Plug &
  Onboard LAN    [Enabled]                    Play O/S is set to No

                                              ▼ <- Indicates that the
                                                    selected device is
                                                    in conflict with
                                                    another device

                                              ↔ Select Screen
                                              ↑↓ Select Item
                                              Enter Select ► Sub-Menu
                                              F1    General Help
                                              F9    Setup Defaults
                                              F10   Save and Exit
                                              ESC   Exit
```

4. Select the **Onboard Audio** option, then press Enter.

5. Use the Up arrow to select **Disabled**. Press Enter.

6. Set the **Onboard LAN** option to disabled.

7. Press the Escape key to return to the Advanced menu.

8. Use the Down arrow key to select the **Video Configuration** sub menu, then press Enter.

   What options can you set in this sub menu?

   _____

9. Make sure that **Onboard Video** is highlighted and press Enter.

10. Use the Up arrow to highlight **Disabled**, then press Enter.

11. Press F10 to save the changes and exit the BIOS.

2.2.4 CONNECT POWER AND CASE CABLES

Scenario

You have just installed a motherboard. Connect the necessary power supply cables to the motherboard. Also, connect the system case's front panel switches, front panel LEDs, and speaker cables to the motherboard. Consult the motherboard documentation as necessary.

Steps

Some system cases combine the individual switch, LED, and speaker cables into one or more larger cables. Other system cases use individual cables for each switch, LED, or speaker. In a case like this, consult the motherboard documentation to find where each cable belongs. In this lab, you will need to identify the identify components by sight and read the documentation to find the correct component to install.

Complete the following steps:

1. In the Workbench, click the **Motherboard** button.

2. Click the **Details** link for the motherboard. Use the documentation to locate the main power supply connector.

   Where is it located?

   _____

3. Drag the correct connector plug from Workbench Connections to the main power connector on the motherboard.

4. Use the motherboard documentation to locate the 12 V power connector.

   Where is it located?

   _____

5. Drag the correct connector plug from Workbench Connections to the 12 V power connector on the motherboard.

6.   Use the motherboard documentation to locate the connectors for the front panel switches.

Where are they located?

_____

What are the names of the front panel switches?

_____

7.   In Workbench Connections, scroll down to find the System Case connectors and drag the front panel switch connectors to their appropriate pins.

8.   Use the motherboard documentation to locate the connectors for the front panel LEDs.

9.   Drag the front panel LED connectors to their appropriate pins.

10. Use the motherboard documentation to locate the speaker cable connector.

11. Drag the speaker connector to its appropriate pins.

2.3.3 CHOOSE A MOTHERBOARD 1

Scenario

You are building a computer for a customer. The customer has the following requirements:

* 1.8 GHz or greater Pentium 4 or Athlon XP processor

* A disk system that supports 100 MB/s or greater data transfer rates (UltraATA/100 or faster)

* At least two integrated USB 2.0 ports

* Integrated stereo sound, including an integrated game port

Click **Details** to examine the specifications of each motherboard on the Shelf. Then choose and install the best motherboard to meet the customer's requirements.

Steps

In this lab, you need to read the specifications of the motherboards and choose a motherboard that supports the required features.

Complete the following steps:

1. In the Shelf, click the **Details** link for each motherboard. Read the documentation and complete the following table to identify the motherboard that meets the scenario requirements. **Note:** When you restart the lab, the motherboard groups will be randomized. If you exit and restart the lab, the correct motherboard might be in a different position.

Motherboard	Socket Type	Processor Speed	ATA Support	USB Support	Sound/Game Port
Group 1					
Group 2					
Group 3					
Group 4					
Group 5					

Which socket types support Pentium 4 or Athlon XP processors?

_____

2. In the Workbench, click the **Motherboard** button to view the motherboard plate inside the system case (this is the Motherboard view).

3. Drag the motherboard from the Shelf and drop it on the system case motherboard plate on the Workbench.

2.3.4 CHOOSE A MOTHERBOARD 2

Scenario

You are building a computer for a customer. The customer has the following requirements:

- 2 GHz or greater Pentium 4 or Athlon XP processor.

- A memory system that supports DDR memory.

- A disk system that supports the latest Serial ATA disks, as well as earlier parallel ATA devices.

- A graphics system that supports AGP 8x.

- An I/O system that supports Firewire (IEEE 1394) ports.

Click **Details** to examine the specifications of each motherboard on the Shelf. Then choose and install the best motherboard to meet the customer's requirements.

Steps

The motherboard documentation provides an overview of the specific motherboard components as well as sections that document the front panel connectors, processor, and memory. You need to read each section to find specific information about these key motherboard components. In this lab, you will need to read the documentation to find the correct component to install.

Complete the following steps:

1. Click the **Details** link for each motherboard. Read the documentation and complete the following table to identify the motherboard that meets the scenario requirements. **Note:** When you restart the lab, the motherboard groups will be randomized. If you exit and restart the lab, the correct motherboard might be in a different position.

Motherboard	Processor	Memory	Disk Drive	Graphics	IEEE 1394 (FireWire)
Group 1					
Group 2					
Group 3					
Group 4					
Group 5					

If you install three memory chips with speeds of 200 MHz, 200 MHz, and 133 MHz, at what speed does your memory run?

_____

2. Switch to Motherboard view.

3. Drag the appropriate motherboard from the Shelf and drop it on the system case motherboard plate.

2.3.5 INSTALL HEADER DEVICES

Scenario

You are setting up a new computer and you have just installed the motherboard. You now need to add components to the motherboard. Your task in this lab is to do the following:

- Install the following port inserts in the system case:

    ○ FireWire

    ○ USB

    ○ eSATA

- Connect the cables for each port insert to the motherboard. Consult the motherboard documentation to identify the correct motherboard connectors.

Steps

Unlike traditional expansion cards, port inserts do not occupy a slot on the motherboard. Rather, the data transfers occur through the data cables and headers. In this lab, you will need to read the motherboard documentation to locate the correct header for each port insert cable connector.

Complete the following steps:

1. In the Shelf, drop a port insert over an open expansion card slot, as if you were installing it into the open slot. The port insert connector cable moves to Workbench Connections.

   How does the installation of port inserts affect the use of expansion cards?

   _____

2. Repeat step 1 for the other port insert.

3. Click the **Motherboard** button.

4. Use the motherboard documentation to locate the following headers:
   - Serial ATA (SATA)
   - IEEE 1394
   - USB

5. In Workbench Connections, drag the cable connector for the SATA port insert to the appropriate header on the motherboard.

6. Repeat step 5 for the USB/Firewire port insert cable connectors.

2.3.6 CONFIGURE MOTHERBOARD JUMPERS

Scenario

You just moved a motherboard from another computer into a new system case. The prior system case had front panel audio connectors, but the new case does not. Because the new case does not have front panel audio connectors, you are planning on using the audio connectors on the back of the motherboard. Consult the motherboard documentation and configure the jumpers so the audio uses the rear ports.

Steps

In this lab, you will need to read the motherboard documentation to identify the exact method used by this motherboard to use the audio connectors on the back of the motherboard.

Complete the following steps:

1. Switch to Motherboard view.

2. Use the motherboard documentation to locate the jumper block to configure the audio connectors.

   What is the jumper block labeled?

   _____

   How many pins are in the jumper block? (You can view the number of pins after you remove the jumper from the pins.)

   _____

3. Zoom in on the motherboard and locate the jumper block for the audio connections.

4. Drag the correct number of jumper plugs from the Shelf to the correct pin positions.

2.3.7 CLEAR THE CMOS

Scenario

You just installed a used motherboard that you purchased online. You have tried to go into the CMOS setup program to make some processor related configurations, but the CMOS is password protected.

To clear the CMOS password, take the following actions:

- Unplug the computer from the wall power.

- Consult the motherboard documentation to identify the motherboard jumper location and position that clears the CMOS.

- Move the jumper to the appropriate location. (On a live system, you would move the jumper back to its original location. In the lab, leave it in the position to clear the CMOS.)

Note: The computer is currently off.

Steps

For most motherboards, you clear the CMOS password by removing or moving a jumper. In this lab, you will need to read the motherboard documentation to identify the exact method used by this motherboard to clear the CMOS password.

Complete the following steps:

1. To unplug the system in the Workbench, drag the power plug in the wall outlet to Workbench Connections.

2. Switch to Motherboard view.

3. Place the mouse over the motherboard. In the popup window, click the **Details** link to view the motherboard documentation.

4. Scroll down to locate the section titled **Clear CMOS Jumper (JBAT1)**.

   According to the documentation, how do you clear the CMOS password?

   _____

   _____

   What is the normal pin location for this jumper?

   _____

   Where is pin 1 located (top, bottom, or middle)?

   _____

5. In the motherboard documentation, scroll up to the motherboard component diagram. Locate the CMOS jumper.

    What is the jumper label?

    _____

    Where is the jumper located?

    _____

6. Zoom in on the motherboard and locate the jumper block for the CMOS.

7. Drag the jumper plug to the correct pin positions to clear the CMOS. (**Note:** On a live system, you would move the jumper back to its original location. In the lab, leave it in the position to clear the CMOS.)

2.4.5 CHOOSE A PROCESSOR 1

Scenario

You are building a computer from some spare computer parts. You are using a motherboard that accepts Intel Pentium 4 processors. You want to install the fastest Intel Pentium 4 processor in your inventory that is fully supported by the motherboard. Open the motherboard's **Details** and read its documentation. Also, click **Details** to read each processor's specifications. Then choose and install the correct processor.

Note: For this lab, you will skip the step of installing a CPU fan.

Steps

The type of processor you can install depends in large part on the support provided by the motherboard. In this lab, you will need to read the motherboard documentation to identify characteristics of the supported processors. Then you will need to read the processor documentation to select the one supported by the motherboard that meets the scenario requirements.

Complete the following steps:

1. Start by identifying the processors supported by the motherboard. In the Workbench, switch to Motherboard view.

2. View the motherboard documentation and complete the following table.

Motherboard Specification	Support
Socket Type	
Core Frequency	
Bus Frequency	
Clock	

How do you configure the motherboard with processor-specific settings?

_____

3. In the motherboard documentation, scroll up to the motherboard component diagram. Locate the processor socket.

    What is the processor socket number in the diagram?

    _____

    Where is the processor socket located?

    _____

4. In the Shelf, view the Details for each processor to read its documentation and complete the following table. **Note:** When you restart the lab, the processor groups will be randomized. If you exit and restart the lab, the correct processor might be in a different position.

Group #	Socket Type	Core Frequency	Bus Frequency	Clock
Group 1				
Group 2				
Group 3				
Group 4				
Group 5				

5. Select the processor that is supported by the motherboard and drag it from the Shelf to the motherboard socket.

2.4.6 CHOOSE A PROCESSOR 2

Scenario

You are building a computer from some spare computer parts. You want to install the newest and fastest processor in your inventory that is fully supported by the motherboard. Open the motherboard's **Details** and read its documentation. Also, click **Details** to read each processor's specifications. Then choose and install the correct processor.

Note: For this lab, you will skip the step of installing a CPU fan.

Steps

Manufacturing technology refers to the denseness of the circuitry on the chip. Newer processors offer smaller manufacturing technologies, simultaneously decreasing costs and increasing capabilities. In this lab, you will need to read the motherboard documentation to identify characteristics of the supported processors. Then you will need to read the processor documentation to select the one supported by the motherboard that meets the scenario requirements.

Complete the following steps:

1. Start by identifying the processors supported by the motherboard. In the Workbench, switch to Motherboard view.

2. View the motherboard documentation to complete the following table.

Motherboard Specification	Support
Socket Type	
Core Frequency	
Bus Frequency	
Clock	

3. In the motherboard documentation, scroll up to the motherboard component diagram. Locate the processor socket.

4. In the Shelf, view the Details for each processor to read its documentation and complete the following table. **Note:** When you restart the lab, the processor groups will be randomized. If you exit and restart the lab, the correct processor might be in a different position.

Group #	Socket Type	Core Frequency	Bus Frequency	Clock	Manufacturing Technology
Group 1					
Group 2					
Group 3					
Group 4					

5. Select the processor that is supported by the motherboard and drag it from the Shelf to the motherboard socket.

2.4.7 INSTALL A PROCESSOR

Scenario

You are building a computer from some spare computer parts. You want to install the fastest processor in your inventory that is fully supported by the motherboard. Open the motherboard's **Details** and read its documentation. Also, click **Details** to read each processor's specifications. Then choose and install the correct processor.

Note: For this lab, you will skip the step of installing a CPU fan.

Steps

In this lab, you will need to read the motherboard documentation to identify characteristics of the supported processors. Then you will need to read the processor documentation to select the one supported by the motherboard that meets the scenario requirements.

Complete the following steps:

1. Start by identifying the processors supported by the motherboard. In the Workbench, switch to Motherboard view.

2. View the motherboard documentation and complete the following table.

Motherboard Specification	Support
Socket Type	
Core Frequency	
Bus Frequency	
Clock	

3. In the motherboard documentation, scroll up to the motherboard component diagram. Locate the processor socket.

4. In the Shelf, view the Details for each processor to read its documentation and complete the following table. **Note:** When you restart the lab, the processor groups will be randomized. If you exit and restart the lab, the correct processor might be in a different position.

Group #	Socket Type	Core Frequency	Bus Frequency	Clock
Group 1				
Group 2				
Group 3				
Group 4				

5. Select the processor that is supported by the motherboard and drag it from the Shelf to the motherboard socket.

2.4.8 INSTALL A HEATSINK AND FAN

Scenario

You have just installed a CPU. This CPU requires a fan for cooling. Install the correct fan. Consult the motherboard documentation as necessary.

Steps

Complete the following steps:

1. Switch to Motherboard view.

2. Using the motherboard documentation, review the processor specifications to determine which fan to install.

3. Drag the CPU fan you want to install to its mount point on the motherboard. The CPU fan cable connector moves to Workbench Connections.

4. Use the motherboard documentation to locate the CPU fan connector on the motherboard.

5. In the Workbench Connections, drag the CPU fan cable connector to the CPU fan connector on the motherboard.

2.5.6 INSTALL SDRAM MEMORY

Scenario

You are building a computer from some spare computer parts. After consulting the motherboard documentation, you find that the motherboard supports two different types of memory. You want to install SDRAM memory that is compatible with the motherboard.

Your task in this lab is to identify the SDRAM memory available on the Shelf. Install the minimum number of memory modules for a functional computer.

Note: Click **Details** to get a close-up view of each type of memory module. Consult the motherboard's documentation, if necessary.

Steps

In this lab, you will need to use the motherboard documentation to find the correct memory modules. You need to select the correct memory type by sight.

Complete the following steps:

1. Switch to Motherboard view. Read the motherboard documentation to locate the 168-pin DIMM (SDRAM) slots.

    How many modules must be installed to meet the scenario requirements?

    _____

    Which slots should be used?

    _____

2. In Motherboard view, use the Zoom feature to examine the slots.

    How many notches would a memory chip have?

    _____

    Where would the notch(es) be positioned?

    _____

3. Click the **Details** link of each memory in the Shelf. Look for memory with the notch characteristics you have noted.

4. Drag the memory to the correct slot.

2.5.7 SELECT AND INSTALL MEMORY

Scenario

You are building a computer from some spare computer parts. Consult the motherboard documentation to identify the type of memory that should be installed. Then select and install enough modules to have a functioning computer.

Note: Click **Details** to get a close-up view of each type of memory module.

Steps

In this lab, you will need to use the motherboard documentation to find the correct memory modules. You need to select the correct memory type by sight.

Complete the following steps:

1. Switch to Motherboard view. Read the motherboard documentation to locate the memory slots.

    How many modules must be installed to meet the scenario requirements?

    _____

    Which slots should be used?

    _____

2. In Motherboard view, use the Zoom feature to examine the slots.

    How many notches would a memory chip have?

    _____

    Where would the notch(es) be positioned?

    _____

3. Click the **Details** link of each memory in the Shelf. Look for memory with the notch characteristics you have noted.

4. Drag the memory to the correct slot.

2.5.8 INSTALL RDRAM MEMORY

Scenario

You are building a computer from some spare computer parts. The motherboard you are working with uses RDRAM (Rambus) memory modules. You want to install 1 GB of memory. You have various memory modules in your inventory on the Shelf. Each module has a capacity of 512 MB.

Consult the motherboard documentation to identify how memory is to be installed. Select and install the memory necessary to meet the requirements.

Note: Click **Details** to get a close-up view of each type of memory module.

Steps

In this lab, you will need to select the correct memory modules by sight. You will also need to consult the motherboard documentation to find the correct installation procedure for optimizing memory performance.

Complete the following steps:

1. Switch to Motherboard view. Read the motherboard documentation to locate the memory slots.

    How many modules must be installed to meet the scenario requirements?

    _____

    Which slots should be used?

    _____

    According to the documentation, what must you do with unused slots?

    _____

2. In Motherboard view, use the Zoom feature to examine the slots.

    How many notches would a memory chip have?

    _____

    Where would the notch(es) be positioned?

    _____

3. Click the **Details** link of each memory in the Shelf. Look for memory with the notch characteristics you have noted.

    What other unique physical characteristics does the memory module have?

    _____

    How can you identify continuity modules?

    _____

4. Drag the modules to the correct slots.

2.5.9 SELECT SDRAM MEMORY

Scenario

You want to install the maximum amount of memory that can be used by this computer. You want to use the fastest performing memory supported by the motherboard. Consult the motherboards' documentation, then choose and install the appropriate memory modules.

Steps

In this lab, you will need to select the correct memory modules by sight after reviewing the motherboard documentation.

Complete the following steps:

1. Switch to Motherboard view. Read the motherboard documentation to locate the memory slots and understand how to configure memory.

    What is the total amount of memory the motherboard supports?

    _____

    What types of memory modules does the motherboard support?

    _____

    How many modules must be installed in pairs? Why?

    _____

    What are acceptable configurations for matching modules?

    _____

2. Click the **Details** button of each memory in the Shelf. Locate the memory you need by completing the table below. **Note:** When you restart the lab, the memory groups will be randomized. If you exit and restart the lab, the correct memory module might be in a different position.

Group #	PC#	Buffered or Unbuffered?	Parity or non-parity (ECC)
Group 1			
Group 2			
Group 3			
Group 4			
Group 5			

3. Drag the amount of required memory to the correct slot.

2.5.10 CHOOSE THE CORRECT MEMORY

Scenario

You want to install as much memory as possible in this computer given the components available in your inventory. Do not use memory modules that are faster or slower than the motherboard supports. Consult the motherboard's documentation, then choose and install the appropriate memory modules.

Steps

In this lab, you will need to select the correct memory modules by sight after reviewing the motherboard documentation.

Complete the following steps:

1. Switch to Motherboard view. Read the motherboard documentation to locate the memory slots and understand how to configure memory.

    What is the total amount of memory the motherboard supports?

    _____

    What types of memory modules does the motherboard support?

    _____

    _____

    What are acceptable configurations for installing memory modules?

    _____

    How many modules must be installed in pairs?

    _____

    What is the disadvantage of installing modules in mixed speeds?

    _____

2. Click the **Details** button of each memory in the Shelf. Locate the memory you need by completing the table below. **Note:** When you restart the lab, the memory groups will be randomized. If you exit and restart the lab, the correct memory module might be in a different position.

Group #	Module memory size (MB) or (GB)	PC Rating	Buffered or Unbuffered?	Registered?	Parity or non-parity (ECC)
Group 1					
Group 2					
Group 3					
Group 4					
Group 5					
Group 6					

3. Drag the amount of required memory to the correct slot.

2.5.11 SELECT DDR MEMORY

Scenario

You want to install 1 GB of memory in this computer. You want the system to perform as fast as possible. Consult the motherboard's documentation, then choose and install the appropriate memory modules.

Steps

In this lab, you will need to select the correct memory modules by sight after reviewing the motherboard documentation.

Complete the following steps:

1. Switch to Motherboard view. Read the motherboard documentation to locate the memory slots and understand how to configure memory.

   What is the total amount of memory the motherboard supports?

   _____

   What types of memory modules does the motherboard support?

   _____

   _____

   What are acceptable configurations for installing memory modules?

   _____

   How many modules must be installed in pairs?

   _____

2. Click the **Details** button of each memory in the Shelf. Locate the memory you need by completing the table below. **Note:** When you restart the lab, the memory groups will be randomized. If you exit and restart the lab, the correct memory module might be in a different position.

Group #	Module memory size (MB) or (GB)	PC Rating	Buffered or Unbuffered?	Registered?	Parity or non-parity (ECC)
Group 1					
Group 2					
Group 3					
Group 4					

3. Drag the amount of required memory to the correct slot.

2.5.12 SELECT RDRAM MEMORY

Scenario

You have several RIMMs in your inventory. You want to install as much memory as possible in this computer as long as all memory runs at the maximum speed supported by the motherboard. Consult the motherboard's documentation, then choose and install the appropriate memory modules.

Steps

Complete the following steps:

1. Switch to Motherboard view. Read the motherboard documentation to locate the memory slots and understand how to configure memory.

    What is the total amount of memory the motherboard supports?

    _____

    What types of memory modules does the motherboard support?

    _____

    _____

    What are acceptable configurations for installing memory modules?

    _____

    How many modules must be installed in pairs? Why?

    _____

    What are the restrictions placed on mixing memory modules?

    _____

2. Click the **Details** button of each memory in the Shelf. Locate the memory you need by completing the table below. **Note:** When you restart the lab, the memory groups will be randomized. If you exit and restart the lab, the correct memory module might be in a different position.

Group #	PC Rating	Buffered or Unbuffered?	Parity or non-parity (ECC)
Group 1			
Group 2			
Group 3			
Group 4			
Group 5			

3. Drag the amount of required memory to the correct slot.

2.5.13 DISABLE MEMORY TESTS

Scenario

A user complains of a computer that counts its memory every time it boots. To speed up the boot process, you want the computer to skip the memory count. Configure the computer appropriately. Remember to save your changes.

Note: If you need to restart the simulated computer, use the Power On/Power Off button in the lower left corner of the lab.

Steps

You can speed up the boot process by enabling Quick Boot mode. This allows the BIOS to skip certain POST routines such as counting extended memory. However, while this speeds up the boot process, it increases the risk of a hardware error going undetected.

Complete the following steps:

1. Press the **F1** key. (If you don't press F1 soon enough, and the computer gives you a DOS prompt, press the Power Off/Power On button in the lower left corner of the screen to restart the lab.)

2. Use the Right arrow key to select to the **Boot** menu.

3. Use the Down arrow key to select **QuickBoot Mode**, then press Enter.

4. Use the Down arrow key to select **Enabled**, then press Enter.

5. Press F10.

6. Press Enter to save the changes and exit.

2.6.4 INSTALL AN AGP CARD

Scenario

You are building a computer from some spare computer parts. You want to install an AGP video adapter in this computer. Click **Details** to see a close-up of each card. Then choose and install the correct expansion card. Do not install any unnecessary cards.

Note: For this lab, you do not need to connect any cables or perform any other hardware configuration besides installing the video adapter.

Steps

In this lab, you will need to select the correct expansion card by sight.

Complete the following steps:

1. Switch to Motherboard view and read the documentation to locate the correct slot on the motherboard.

    What characteristics does the slot have that give you clues about what the card must look like to fit in to the slot?

    _____

2. In the Shelf, locate the card that corresponds to the expansion slot and meets the scenario requirements. Use the Details link to examine each card as necessary.

    How do the contacts on the card's connecting tabs differ on the correct card from those on the other cards?

    _____

3. Drag the appropriate card to the appropriate slot on the motherboard.

2.6.5 INSTALL AN EXPANSION CARD

Scenario

You are in the process of creating a new computer. Your motherboard provides onboard support for peripheral devices, but you would rather use the increased capabilities of expansion cards for some of your peripherals.

Your task in this lab is to install the following expansion cards:

- Video card

- Network card

- Modem

Select cards that are supported by the motherboard bus types.

Steps

In this lab, you will need to choose the correct expansion cards by sight. To do this, you need to visually recognize characteristics of the PCI and newer PCIe standards.

Complete the following steps:

1. In the Workbench, examine the motherboard. Answer the following questions:

   What type of slot is most common on the motherboard?

   _____

   What are common characteristics of a card that fits into this type of slot?

   _____

   How are the slots that are not among the most common type similar to the most common type?

   _____

   What does this tell you about these other slots?

   _____

   Examine the longest orange slot with the connector lock at the end. How many contacts would the connector tab have on the type of card that fits into this slot?

   _____

   How does knowing the answer to the previous question help you decide what type of card to choose from the Shelf?

   _____

2. In the Shelf, drag the following cards to the appropriate slots on the motherboard:
   - Video card
   - Network card
   - Modem

   (**Hint:** Look for cards that have connectors that look like the same size as the slots into which they fit.)

2.7.4 SELECT AN AGP CARD

Scenario

You are building a computer from some spare computer parts. You want to install the fastest AGP video adapter that is fully supported by the computer's motherboard. You want to reserve faster video cards for other computers you are planning to build, even though such cards might work in this motherboard at a slower speed. Choose and install an AGP expansion card that meets these requirements.

Tip: Consult the motherboard documentation to identify supported video cards.

Steps

In this lab, you will need to read the specifications for each card to find the correct card to install.

Complete the following steps:

1. In the Shelf, read the specifications for each card and complete the table below to identify the card that meets the scenario requirements. **Note:** When you restart the lab, the card groups will be randomized. If you exit and restart the lab, the correct group might be in a different position.

Group #	Speed (#x)	Voltage	Motherboard support (Yes or No)
Group 1			
Group 2			
Group 3			
Group 4			
Group 5			

2. Drag the appropriate card to the AGP slot on the motherboard.

2.7.5 UPGRADE A VIDEO CARD

Scenario

You want to install a video card to support dual digital LCD monitors and component TV video out. You can only afford the video card right now, so you need to continue using your current CRT monitor. Your task in this lab is to do the following:

- Disconnect the monitor by dragging the connector from its current location to the Shelf.

- Install a new video card with as much memory as possible while allowing TV out with component video.

- Connect the monitor to the new video card using the appropriate cables.

Steps

In this lab, you need to read the specifications for each card to find the correct card to install. You will also need to recognize the correct connectors by sight.

Complete the following steps:

1. In the Workbench, drag the monitor cable connector to the Shelf to disconnect the monitor.

2. Click the **Motherboard** button.

3. In the Shelf, click the **Expansion Cards** category.

4. In the Shelf, read the specifications for each card and complete the table below to identify the card that meets the scenario requirements. **Note:** When you restart the lab, the card groups will be randomized. If you exit and restart the lab, the correct group might be in a different position.

Group #	Card Type (e.g., AGP)	Memory (e.g., 256 MB)	Component TV out?	Connection Ports
Group 1				
Group 2				
Group 3				
Group 4				
Group 5				
Group 6				

How can you tell the difference between component TV out and S-video TV out?

_____

5. In the Shelf, drag the appropriate card to the appropriate slot on the motherboard. (Use the motherboard documentation as necessary to identify a slot.)

6. Switch to Back view by clicking the **Back** button.

7. Click the **Cables** category.

    What type of cable will you use to connect the CRT monitor?

_____

8. Drag the appropriate connector to the connector on the video card. (Examine the port on the card and the cable connectors to identify a connector.) The other connector moves to Workbench Connections.

9. In Workbench Connections, drag the video cable connector to the port on the monitor.

    What type of connectors should the video card have to support dual digital monitors as well as your current CRT monitor?

_____

2.7.6 SELECT A DUAL MONITOR VIDEO CARD

Scenario

Your current system uses an AGP video card and a CRT monitor. A friend has recently given you a second CRT monitor, and you want to connect it to your computer in a dual monitor configuration. You know that you need to purchase a new video card and possibly some cables, but you'd like to keep the cost down as low as possible.

Your task in this lab is to do the following:

- Uninstall the current monitor and video card. You will need to disconnect the current monitor, then drag the card from its current location and drop it onto the Shelf.

- Install a new video card with the lowest cost while allowing you to connect both monitors.

- Connect both monitors to the video card using the appropriate cables.

Steps

In this lab, you'll need to recognize DVI-I connectors by sight and identify cables by name. You'll also need to recognize acceptable dual monitor configurations.

Complete the following steps:

1. In the Workbench, drag the monitor connector that is connected to the existing video card to Workbench Connections.

   What kind of connector does the monitor use?

   _____

   How will this affect your choice of video card and cables?

   _____

2. Switch to Motherboard view by clicking the **Motherboard** button.

3. Remove the existing video card by dragging the video adapter card to the Shelf.

4. In the Shelf, read the specifications and click the **Details** button for each card to complete the table below to identify the card that meets the scenario requirements. **Note:** When you restart the lab, the card groups will be randomized. If you exit and restart the lab, the correct group might be in a different position.

Group #	Price	Available Connectors
Group 1		
Group 2		
Group 3		

5. Click the **Cables** category. Read the specifications for each cable to complete the table below to identify the cable that meets the scenario requirements. **Note:** When you restart the lab, the cable groups will be randomized. If you exit and restart the lab, the correct group might be in a different position.

Group #	Cable Type	Price	Connectors
Group 1			
Group 2			
Group 3			
Group 4			

6. Click the **Expansion Cards** category.

7. Drag the appropriate video adapter card to an appropriate expansion slot on the motherboard.

8. Click the **Back** button.

9. Drag the connector in Workbench Connections to the appropriate port on the video adapter card.

10. Click the **Cables** category.

11. Drag the appropriate cable connector to the open port on the expansion card. The other connector moves to Workbench Connections.

12. Drag the connector in Workbench Connections to the port on the second monitor.

2.7.9 INCREASE SHARED VIDEO MEMORY

Scenario

Your desktop computer has a video card built into the motherboard. To improve video performance, increase the amount of shared video memory 64 MB.

Steps

Complete the following steps.

1. To enter the CMOS setup, press F1.

2. Press the Right arrow key to select the **Advanced** menu.

3. Use the Down arrow key to select the **Video Configuration** sub menu. Press Enter.

    What is the current amount of shared video memory?

    _____

4. Use the Down arrow to select the shared memory option and press Enter.

5. Use the Down arrow to select the setting designated by the scenario, then press Enter.

6. Press F10 to save the changes and press Enter to exit.

2.7.10 SET THE AGP APERTURE

Scenario

You have a customer who has complained that when he plays games on his computer, the graphics occasionally pause and glitch. Increase the AGP aperture to 128 MB.

Steps

Complete the following steps:

1.   To enter the CMOS setup, press F1.

2.   Press the Right arrow key to select the **Advanced** menu.

3.   Use the Down arrow key to select the **Video Configuration** sub menu. Press Enter.

4.   Use the Down arrow to select the aperture size configuration and press Enter.

5.   Use the Down arrow to select the setting designated by the scenario, then press Enter.

6.   Press F10 to save the changes and press Enter to exit.

2.8.4 INSTALL A SOUND CARD

Scenario

You have just purchased a new sound card for your computer. Your task in this lab is to:

- Install the sound card in a free expansion slot.

- Connect the sound card CD port to the CD-ROM drive. (Consult the sound card documentation to identify the port location.)

- Connect the speakers and the microphone to the sound card.

- Connect the speakers to the power outlet.

Steps

In this lab, you will need to read the documentation (when available) to find the correct components to install. You will also need to select cables and components by sight.

Complete the following steps:

1. Switch to Motherboard view.

2. In the Shelf, click the **Expansion Cards** category.

3. Drag the sound card to an open PCI slot on the motherboard.

4. With the sound card installed, you must connect it to both the CD-ROM drive and the microphone. Begin by clicking the **Cables** category and dragging an MPC connector similar to the MPC connector you see below to the TAD I/O port on the sound card. (To locate the TAD I/O port, click **Details** for the sound card, then click the **Documentation** tab to find the sound card components.) The other connector moves to Workbench Connections.

5. Click **Drive Bays.**

6. To connect the sound card to the CD-ROM drive, drag the cable connector in Workbench Connections to the Analog Audio port on the CD-ROM drive. (Again, click **Details** for the CD-ROM drive, then click the **Documentation** tab to find the CD-ROM drive components.)

7. Click the **Back** button.

8. In the Shelf, click the **Speakers** category.

9. Drag the speaker connector to the sound card's Line Out port (click the **Details** link and **Documentation** tab as necessary to locate the correct port).

10. Because the speakers need power, you must connect them to the electric outlet. Click the **Cables** category and drag the power connector for the speakers to the port on the back of the left speaker. The electric plug moves to Workbench Connections.

11. Drag the plug from Workbench Connections to the electric outlet.

12. To connect the microphone, in the Shelf drag the microphone connector to the sound card's microphone port.

2.8.5 SELECT A SOUND CARD

Scenario

You are building a new computer. You want the computer to support a speaker system with left front, center front, right front, left rear, right rear, and subwoofer speakers. The computer has a DVD drive and DVD movies will be played in it. You want to make sure that the audio signal is decoded at the sound card or speakers. Install the best sound card to meet these requirements. Make the necessary connection between the DVD drive and the sound card. Consult the sound card documentation as necessary.

Steps

Different sound cards support different speaker configurations. Basic stereo speakers are known as a 2.0 system. If a subwoofer is included to intensify the low frequencies, the system is known as a 2.1 speaker system. If right and left rear speakers are added, the system becomes a 4.1 system. If a front center channel is added, the system becomes a 5.1 system, and if a rear center channel is added, the system is known as a 6.1 system.

In this lab, you will need to read the specifications to identify the correct card to install.

Complete the following steps:

1. In the Shelf, read the specifications for each sound card and complete the table below to identify the card that meets the scenario requirements. **Note:** When you restart the lab, the card groups will be randomized. If you exit and restart the lab, the correct group might be in a different position.

Group #	Speaker System Supported	Output (Analog or Digital)	# of Voices Supported	Frequency Response Range
Group 1				
Group 2				
Group 3				

2. Click the **Motherboard** button and drag the appropriate card from the Shelf to an empty PCI slot on the motherboard.

3. To take full advantage of the sound card's capabilities, connect it to the DVD drive's SPDIF port. To do this, click the **Cables** category and drag the appropriate cable connector to the SPDIF port on the sound card. (To locate the SPDIF port, click the sound card's **Details** then **Documentation** tab to locate sound card's components.) The other connector moves to Workbench Connections.

4. Switch to Drive Bays view.

5. Drag the connector in Workbench Connections to the SPDIF port on the DVD drive. (Again, use the drive's **Details** and **Documentation** tab to find the SPDIF port.)

3.0
Storage Devices

3.1.4 INSTALL A FLOPPY DRIVE

Scenario

You are building a computer for a customer. The customer wants a standard 3.5 inch floppy drive as Drive A. Install a floppy drive in this computer using the proper cabling.

Steps

On a typical floppy drive ribbon cable, seven wires are twisted to opposite positions prior to the connector that will be used for drive A. The connector furthest from the twisted wires is intended to be connected to the motherboard.

Complete the following steps:

1. Click the **Drive Bays** button.

2. Drag the floppy disk drive to an open drive bay of the appropriate size.

3. In the Shelf, click the **Details** link for each cable. Examine each cable and complete the table below to identify the cable that meets the scenario requirements. **Note:** When you restart the lab, the cable groups will be randomized. If you exit and restart the lab, the correct group might be in a different position.

Group #	# of Pins	# of Connectors	Twist
Group 1			
Group 2			
Group 3			
Group 4			

4. Drag the appropriate floppy disk drive cable connector to the appropriate location on the floppy disk. The other connector moves to Workbench Connections.

5. Switch to Motherboard view.

6. In Workbench Connections, drag the unconnected floppy disk drive cable connector to the appropriate location on the motherboard (click the **Details** link for the motherboard and consult the documentation as necessary to locate the connector).

7. Switch back to Drive Bays view.

8. In Workbench Connections, drag an appropriate power connector to the power connector on the floppy disk drive.

3.1.5 INSTALL TWO FLOPPY DRIVES

Scenario

You are building a computer from some spare parts. The computer will be used to perform driver installation tests from floppy disks. You want the computer to have two floppy drives, so you can perform the tests from both drive A and drive B. You have an old floppy drive that you removed from another computer, and a new floppy drive that you purchased especially for this computer. You want to install both floppy drives. Install the new floppy drive as drive A and the old floppy drive as drive B.

Hint: The old floppy drive has a Drive Select jumper that can be set to DS0 (Drive A) or DS1 (Drive B). The DS0 position is on the left.

Steps

In this lab, you will need to select the correct drives and cables by sight.

Complete the following steps:

1. Switch to Drive Bays view.

2. In the Shelf, drag the new floppy disk drive to the upper 3.5 drive bay.

    Why would you want the new drive to be above the old drive?

    _____

3. Drag the old floppy disk drive to the lower 3.5 drive bay.

4. In the Workbench, locate the drive selector jumper on the old floppy disk drive. Set the jumper to make the old drive the B drive. (Use the Zoom In feature to magnify your view of the drive. Click **Details** for the drive and then the **Documentation** tab to find the correct jumper position.)

    What is the relationship between the position of this jumper and the twist in a standard floppy disk drive cable?

    _____

5. In the Shelf, drag the appropriate floppy disk drive cable connector to the connector on the new floppy disk drive. The other connectors move to Workbench Connections.

    How many connectors must the cable have to complete this installation?

    _____

    Where should you install the connector farthest from the twist in the cable?

    _____

6. In Workbench Connections, drag the appropriate floppy disk drive cable connector to the connector on the old floppy disk drive.

7. To complete the drive installation, you must provide power to them. Drag floppy disk power connectors to the power pins on each of the floppy disk drives.

8. With the drives installed, you must connect them to the motherboard. To do so, switch to Motherboard view.

9. In Workbench Connections, drag the floppy disk cable connector to the floppy disk drive connector socket on the motherboard.

3.2.4 INSTALL A PATA HARD DISK

Scenario

You are building a computer from some spare parts. You have a used hard drive that you want to use as the computer's boot disk. Complete the following steps:

1. Install the hard drive into an appropriate drive bay.

2. Click **Details** to view a close up of each cable. Then choose the proper cable and use it to connect the hard drive to the motherboard's primary IDE interface. Consult the motherboard documentation, if necessary.

3. Consult the hard drive's documentation. Then zoom in to the back of the hard drive and jumper the hard drive appropriately.

4. Provide an appropriate power source for the hard drive.

Note: In the future, you are planning on installing a floppy disk drive and an internal ZIP drive into this computer.

Steps

In this lab, you will need to read the documentation to find the proper method of installation for the components.

Complete the following steps:

1. To begin, switch to Drive Bays view.

2. In the Shelf, click the **Hard Drives** category and drag the hard drive to a drive bay.

3. In the Workbench, use the Zoom In feature to magnify your view of the hard disk drive cable connector.

    How many pins does the connector have?

    _____

4. In the Shelf, drag the appropriate hard drive cable connector to the connector on the hard disk drive. (Click the **Details** link for each cable as necessary to determine which cable fits the hard disk drive connector.)

    What's the difference between the hard drive cable and a floppy drive cable?

    _____

5. With the hard disk drive in place, you can set the jumpers to make this the boot disk drive. Click the **Details** link for the drive. Read the documentation and complete the table below to determine how to jumper the drive properly. (Use a Y for Yes if jumpers must be placed over the pins to activate a specific setting. Use an N for No if the pins must not be connected to activate a specific setting.)

Setting	Pins 1-2	Pins 3-4	Pins 5-6	Pins 7-8
Single Drive				
Dual Drives (Master)				
Dual Drives (Slave)				
Cable Select				

6. In the Shelf, click the **Jumpers** category and drag jumper plugs to the appropriate jumper pins on the hard drive to make it the boot disk drive.

7. With the drive configured as the boot drive, you can supply power to it. In Workbench Connectors, drag the appropriate power connector to the power connector on the hard drive.

8. With the hard disk drive installed, you must connect it to the motherboard. To do this, switch to Motherboard view.

9. Read the motherboard documentation to locate the primary IDE interface on the motherboard.

    How many IDE interfaces are there on the motherboard?

    _____

    How is the primary interface identified?

    _____

10. In Workbench Connections, drag the hard disk drive cable connector to the IDE interface connector on the motherboard.

3.2.5 CONFIGURE DRIVE JUMPERS

Scenario

You just installed two CD/DVD drives in a computer. One drive supports the CD-ROM format only, which you will use to install software and play CD-ROM based games. The other drive supports the CD-R/RW and DVD-ROM formats. You have connected the drives to the motherboard using a 40 conductor ATA (IDE) ribbon cable. You have also provided an appropriate power source. Now you need to configure the drives.

Consult each drive's documentation. Jumper the drive in the upper drive bay as Master, and jumper the drive in the lower drive bay as Slave.

Note: In this lab, you jumper the drives after installing them into a bay. However, in real life it is usually easier to jumper the drives before installing them into a drive bay. Also, keep in mind that the simulator lets you zoom in to get a better view of the back of the drives.

Steps

When two drives are placed on the same channel, one drive must be configured as Master, and the other drive must be configured as Slave. The Master drive will be detected first, and the Slave drive will be detected second. Furthermore, disks on the primary IDE channel are detected before disks on the secondary IDE channel. Operating systems typically assign drive letters to drives in the order they are detected.

Complete the following steps:

1. To begin, switch to Drive Bays view.

2. In the Workbench, click the **Details** link for the CD-ROM drive. Read the documentation and complete the table below to determine how to jumper the drive properly. (Use a Y for Yes if jumpers must be placed over the pins to activate a specific setting. Use an N for No if the pins must not be connected to activate a specific setting.)

Setting	Pins 1-2	Pins 3-4	Pins 5-6	Pins 7-8	Pins 9-10
Single Drive					
Dual Drives (Master)					
Dual Drives (Slave)					
Cable Select					

3. In the Shelf, drag jumper plugs to the appropriate pins on the CD-ROM drive to jumper the drive according to the scenario requirements.

4. In the Workbench, click the **Details** link for the CD-R/RW and DVD drive. Read the documentation and complete the table below to determine how to jumper the drive properly. (Use a Y for Yes if jumpers must be placed over the pins to activate a specific setting. Use an N for No if the pins must not be connected to activate a specific setting.)

Setting	Pins 1-2	Pins 3-4	Pins 5-6	Pins 7-8	Pins 9-10
Single Drive					
Dual Drives (Master)					
Dual Drives (Slave)					
Cable Select					

5. In the Shelf, drag jumper plugs to the appropriate pins on the CD-R/RW and DVD drive to jumper the drive according to the scenario requirements.

3.2.6 SELECT A HARD DRIVE

Scenario

You are building a new computer for a customer. You want to install the fastest hard drive that is fully supported by the motherboard. Consult the motherboard's documentation, then choose the most appropriate drive. Install the hard drive in an internal drive bay, making sure that the configuration lets the hard drive operate at maximum speeds. Be sure to examine the cables closely to determine the correct cable. Minimize jumper configuration changes, and reserve secondary IDE channels for other devices. Install only one hard drive.

Steps

A couple of notes on cables:

- To use Cable Select, use the color-coded connectors on the cable (it's a good idea to use the color-coded connectors even if you are not using Cable Select).

- Use the black connector for the master drive or a single drive.

- Use the gray connector for a slave drive (if present). Use the blue connector to connect to the controller on the motherboard.

- A 40-pin, 80-conductor UltraATA ribbon cable allows a drive to achieve UltraATA/66 and faster speeds where a 40-conductor cable only allows the drive to operate at UltraATA/33 speeds.

Complete the following steps:

1. To begin, click the **Motherboard** button and click the **Details** link for the motherboard. Read the documentation and complete the table below to identify the drive that meets the scenario requirements..

Motherboard IDE Connector	Name and Speed (e.g., UltraATA/33)	Color/Location	Channel
1			
2			
3			
4			

How do you distinguish primary from secondary channels?

_____

What is the maximum IDE drive speed the motherboard supports?

_____

2. Switch to Drive Bays view.

3. In the Shelf, click the **Hard Drives** category and drag a hard drive that meets the scenario requirements to an internal drive bay.

4. Click the **Cables** category and drag the appropriate hard drive cable connector to the connector on the back of the hard drive.

5. In Workbench Connections, drag a power connector to the power receptacle on the hard disk drive. (Use the **Details** link and the **Documentation** tab for the hard disk drive as necessary to locate the power receptacle.)

6. With the drive installed, you can connect it to the motherboard. Start by switching to Motherboard view.

7. In Workbench Connections, drag the hard drive cable connector to the appropriate motherboard IDE interface.

   To which IDE interface should you connect it? Why?

   _____

3.2.7 INSTALL AN ULTRA ATA DRIVE

Scenario

You are replacing a computer's hard drive. You have installed a new UltraATA/133 drive into the system case, configured it by keeping the Cable Select setting, and supplied it with appropriate power. Now connect the hard drive to the computer. Ensure that the computer's new disk storage system will operate at maximum speed. Consult the motherboard documentation, if necessary.

Steps

In this lab, you will need to read the documentation to find the correct component to install.

Complete the following steps:

1. To begin, click the **Motherboard** button and click the **Details** link for the motherboard.

   What is the maximum IDE drive speed supported by the motherboard? Why is this unacceptable?

   _____

   _____

2. In the Shelf, click the **Details** link for each expansion card. Examine each card and complete the table below to identify the card that meets the scenario requirements. **Note:** When you restart the lab, the card groups will be randomized. If you exit and restart the lab, the correct group might be in a different position.

Group #	Name and Speed	# of Ports	Expansion Slot Type
Group 1			
Group 2			
Group 3			

3. Drag the appropriate expansion slot to an open slot on the motherboard.

4. Now that you've installed a card that can support the drive's speed, you need to connect the card and the drive. To do this, switch to Drive Bays view.

5. In the Shelf, drag a hard drive cable to the hard drive's connector. The other connector moves to Workbench Connections.

6. Switch back to Motherboard view.

7. In Workbench Connections, drag the hard drive cable connector to the appropriate connector on the expansion card.

3.3.4 INSTALL SATA DRIVES

Scenario

You are building a machine for the video editor in your company. He has requested that you install fast hard drives that provide a large amount of space for storing large video files. Your task in this lab is to install two SATA drives in the computer using the appropriate data and power cables.

Steps

In this lab, you will need to identify serial ATA (SATA) drives and their components by sight.

Complete the following steps:

1. Click the **Drive Bays** view button.

2. In the Shelf, click **Details** to view each drive.

    How can you tell the difference between SATA drives and other drives?

    _____

3. Drag both SATA drives to the appropriate drive bays.

4. Click the **Cables** category.

5. Click **Details** to help you select the correct cable.

6. Drag the appropriate cable connectors to the data ports on both drives. The other connectors move to Workbench Connections.

7. In Workbench Connections, drag the appropriate power connectors to the power ports on the backs of both drives.

8. In the Workbench, click the **Motherboard** button.

9. In Workbench Connections, drag the other data cable connectors to the SATA headers on the motherboard.

3.4.5 INSTALL A SCSI ADAPTER AND DEVICE

Scenario

You have a SCSI CD drive that you want to connect to a computer. Choose and install a SCSI adapter that will fully support the drive. Then connect the CD drive to the computer using the most appropriate cable. Power the CD drive appropriately. Keep the SCSI adapter's default configuration (SCSI ID 7 and auto terminated), but configure the CD drive to operate properly on the SCSI bus. Consult the documentation for the SCSI adapter and the CD drive as necessary.

Note: In the lab, you can zoom in to get a better view of the drive.

Steps

In this lab, you will need to read the documentation to find the correct components to install.

Complete the following steps:

1. In the Shelf, click the **CD-DVD Drives** category and drag the drive to the desktop.

   What SCSI variety is the drive?

   _____

2. In the Shelf, click the **Details** link for each expansion card. Examine each card and complete the table below to identify the card that meets the scenario requirements. **Note:** When you restart the lab, the card groups will be randomized. If you exit and restart the lab, the correct group might be in a different position.

Group #	SCSI Variety (e.g., Fast Single Wide)	# of Ports	Termination Required? (Y/N)	Expansion Slot Type
Group 1				
Group 2				
Group 3				
Group 4				
Group 5				

3. In the Workbench, switch to Motherboard view.

4. In the Shelf, drag the card to an open slot on the motherboard.

   Of the cards that support the drive's SCSI variety, what makes the card that does not require termination the correct choice?

   _____

5. In the Workbench, switch to Back view.

6. In the Shelf, click the **Cables** category and drag the appropriate cable to the SCSI connector on the back of the computer. (Use the Zoom In feature as necessary to magnify your view of the connectors.) The other connector moves to Workbench Connections.

7. In Workbench Connections, drag the SCSI connector to a connector on the back of the SCSI drive.

8. In the Shelf, drag the appropriate power plug to the power receptacle on the back of the SCSI drive.

9. In Workbench Connections, drag the power plug to the electrical outlet.

10. With the expansion card and drive installed, you need to configure the drive to work properly in the SCSI chain. To do this, you need to set the SCSI drive's ID.

    What is the SCSI card's ID?

    _____

    Because you cannot use the SCSI card's ID, which IDs are available to you?

    _____

11. In the Workbench, magnify the view of the SCSI ID switch and set the drive's SCSI ID to an available ID.

12. With the ID set, you need to terminate the drive because it is the last device in the SCSI chain. However, there are no external terminators available to you, so you must use the drive's onboard terminator. Locate the terminator below the SCSI ID switch and set the **TERM** switch to the **ON** position.

3.4.6 CONNECT EXTERNAL SCSI DEVICES

Scenario

You want to connect a SCSI CD drive and a SCSI scanner to a computer. You have put the CD drive and scanner next to the computer and connected them to a power outlet. Now you need to connect the devices to the computer's SCSI adapter and configure the devices to operate on the SCSI bus.

The SCSI adapter is currently using ID 7 and an internal hard drive is currently using ID 0. Reserve IDs 1, 2, 3, and 4 for future devices. Configure the CD drive to have a higher priority on the SCSI bus than the scanner.

Note: In the lab, you can zoom in to get a better view of the back of the devices.

Steps

In this lab, you must identify the correct components and settings by sight.

Complete the following steps:

1. To begin, switch to Back view.

2. In the Shelf, drag the appropriate cable connector to the SCSI card connector on the back of the computer. (Use the Zoom In feature to magnify your view of the connectors as necessary.) The other connector moves to Workbench Connections.

3. In Workbench Connections, drag the SCSI connector to a SCSI connector on the back of the CD drive.

4. In the Shelf, drag a SCSI cable connector to the open SCSI connector on the CD drive.

5. In Workbench Connections, drag the SCSI cable connector to a SCSI connector on the scanner.

6. With the devices connected, you must now configure their SCSI IDs according to the scenario requirements. In the Workbench, set the SCSI ID on the CD drive to the appropriate ID. (Use the Zoom In feature to magnify your view of the SCSI ID switch on the CD drive as necessary.)

    Note: On a narrow SCSI bus, the order of priority (highest to lowest) is as follows: 7, 6, 5, 4, 3, 2, 1, 0. On a wide SCSI bus, the order of priority (highest to lowest) is as follows: 7, 6, 5, 4, 3, 2, 1, 0, 15, 14, 13, 12, 11, 10, 9, 8.

7. Set the SCSI ID on the scanner to the appropriate ID.

3.4.7 INSTALL AN INTERNAL SCSI DEVICE

Scenario

You are installing a used SCSI hard drive for a computer. In the future, you are planning to upgrade to a faster SCSI drive. To prepare for the future upgrade, choose and install a SCSI adapter that is fully supported by this motherboard and that will fully support the current SCSI hard drive and as many faster SCSI drives as possible. Then install the hard drive and connect it to the computer using the most appropriate cable. Power the hard drive appropriately. Keep the SCSI adapter's default configuration, but be sure to configure the hard drive to operate properly on the SCSI bus.

Note: In the lab, you jumper drives after installing them in a drive bay. In the real world, it is usually easier to jumper drives before installing them.

Steps

In this lab, you must read the documentation to find the correct components to install.

Complete the following steps:

1. To begin, switch to Drive Bays view.

2. In the Shelf, click the **Hard Drives** category and drag the drive to an open drive bay.

    What SCSI variety is the drive?

    _____

3. In the Shelf, open the Expansion Cards category and click the **Details** link for each expansion card. Examine each card and complete the table below to identify the card that meets the scenario requirements. **Note:** When you restart the lab, the card groups will be randomized. If you exit and restart the lab, the correct group might be in a different position.

Group #	SCSI Variety (e.g., Fast Single Wide)	# of Ports	LVD or HVD	Expansion Slot Type
Group 1				
Group 2				
Group 3				
Group 4				
Group 5				
Group 6				

4. In the Workbench, switch to Motherboard view.

5. In the Shelf, drag the card to an open slot on the motherboard.

    How do the scenario requirements make the Ultra2 SCSI card unsuitable for installation?

    _____

6. In the Shelf, open the Cables category and drag a cable connector to the SCSI card connector. The other connector moves to Workbench Connections.

   Which cable has a built-in terminator?

   _____

   What are the advantages to using the self-terminating cable?

   _____

7. In the Workbench, click the **Drive Bays** button.

8. In Workbench Connections, drag the SCSI cable connector to the SCSI connector on the hard drive.

9. Drag a power connector to the power receptacle on the hard drive.

10. With the SCSI drive installed, you must now set the SCSI ID. Click the **Details** for the drive and complete the table below to determine how to set the SCSI ID.

    Which jumper block is already in use? (Use that jumper block to fill in the table and set the SCSI ID.)

    _____

Pins	Setting	Notes

11. Set the hard drive's jumpers to assign the drive a SCSI ID other than 7.

    Which jumper pins did you decide to set plugs on?

    _____

    Based on your jumper pin selection, what is the SCSI ID you assigned to the drive?

    _____

3.5.2 SELECT A CD DRIVE

Scenario

You want a CD drive that can conveniently connect to a computer in a plug and play, hot swappable manner. You will use the CD drive for software installation tasks, so you want the drive to read CD-ROM discs as fast as possible. The drive must also let you write data from computer hard drives to CD-R or CD-RW discs. The computer on your workbench is typical of the computers to which you will connect the drive. Choose and install the most appropriate drive. Power the drive in the most appropriate manner.

Steps

In this lab, you must read the documentation to find the correct components to install.

Complete the following steps:

1. In the Shelf, open the CD-DVD Drives category and click the **Details** link for each drive. Examine each drive and complete the table below to identify the drive that meets the scenario requirements. **Note:** When you restart the lab, the drive groups will be randomized. If you exit and restart the lab, the correct group might be in a different position.

Group #	Connection Type	Speed	Memory	Access Time	R-RW Capable?
Group 1					
Group 2					
Group 3					
Group 4					
Group 5					
Group 6					

2. Drag the appropriate drive to the Workbench.

3. In the Workbench, switch to Back view.

4. In the Shelf, drag an appropriate cable connector to the appropriate port on the back of the drive. The other connector moves to Workbench Connections.

5. In Workbench Connections, drag the cable connector to an appropriate port on the back of the computer (use the Zoom In feature as necessary to locate the port).

6. In the Shelf, drag a power plug to the power receptacle on the back of the drive.

7. In Workbench Connections, drag the power plug to the electrical outlet.

3.5.3 SELECT AN OPTICAL DRIVE

Scenario

You are helping a friend build a computer. Your friend wants to read and write as many types of optical discs as possible. Choose and install the most appropriate drive. Provide appropriate power to the drive and make sure your friend can play CD audio through the motherboard's onboard sound adapter. A hard drive is currently installed in the computer. Install the optical drive in a manner that will not interfere with the computer's hard drive performance. Minimize configuration of the optical drive.

Steps

In this lab, you must read the documentation to find the correct components to install.

Complete the following steps:

1. In the Shelf, open the CD-DVD Drives category and click the **Details** link for each drive. Examine each drive and complete the table below to identify the drive that meets the scenario requirements. **Note:** When you restart the lab, the drive groups will be randomized. If you exit and restart the lab, the correct group might be in a different position.

Group #	Connection Type	Speed	Memory	Access Time	Formats Supported
Group 1					
Group 2					
Group 3					
Group 4					
Group 5					

2. In the Workbench, switch to Drive Bays view.

3. In the Shelf, drag the appropriate drive to an open drive bay.

4. Click the **Cables** category and drag an appropriate cable connector to the appropriate port on the back of the drive. The other connector moves to Workbench Connections.

5. In the Workbench, switch to Motherboard view.

6. In Workbench Connections, drag the connector to the motherboard connector.

7. Click **Details** to locate the CD audio connector, then drag a cable from the Shelf to the connector.

8. Switch to Drive Bays view.

9. In Workbench Connections, drag the CD audio cable connector to the audio connector on the drive.

10. Drag a power connector to the power receptacle on the drive.

3.6.2 SELECT A HARD DRIVE 1

Scenario

You are building a computer from some spare parts. You want to install the fastest hard drive that is fully supported by the motherboard. Consult the motherboard's documentation if necessary. You want the hard drive to have at least a 30 GB capacity, but you would prefer an even greater capacity. Choose and install the most appropriate hard drive. Make only required configuration changes to the hard drive during the installation process.

Note: In this lab, you jumper drives after installing them into a bay. However, in real life it is usually easier to jumper drives before installing them into a drive bay. Also, keep in mind that the simulator lets you zoom in to get a better view of the drive jumpers.

Steps

In this lab, you must read the documentation to find the correct components to install.

Complete the following steps:

1. In the Shelf, open the Hard Drives category and click the **Details** link for each drive. Examine each drive and complete the table below to identify the drive that meets the scenario requirements. **Note:** When you restart the lab, the drive groups will be randomized. If you exit and restart the lab, the correct group might be in a different position.

Group #	Name and Speed	Storage Capacity	RPMs	Connection Type
Group 1				
Group 2				
Group 3				
Group 4				
Group 5				
Group 6				

Which drive is fully supported by the motherboard? (Click **Details** for the motherboard to read the documentation.)

_____

2. In the Workbench, switch to Drive Bays view.

3. In the Shelf, drag the appropriate drive to an open drive bay.

4. Click the **Cables** category and drag an appropriate cable connector to the appropriate port on the back of the drive. The other connector moves to Workbench Connections.

5. In the Workbench, switch to Motherboard view.

6. In Workbench Connections, drag the hard drive's cable connector to the appropriate motherboard connector.

7. Switch back to Drive Bays view and drag a power connector from Workbench Connections to the power receptacle on the drive.

3.6.3 SELECT A HARD DRIVE 2

Scenario

You want a hard drive that can conveniently connect to a computer in a plug and play, hot swappable manner. Currently, you need to store 30 GB of data on the hard drive. You want to minimize the required hardware when installing the hard drive to various computers. The computer on your workbench is typical of the computers to which you will connect the hard drive. Choose and install the most appropriate hard drive. Power the hard drive in the most appropriate manner.

Steps

In this lab, you must read the documentation to find the correct components to install.

Complete the following steps:

1. In the Shelf, open the Hard Drives category and click the **Details** link for each drive. Examine each drive and complete the table below to identify the drive that meets the scenario requirements. **Note:** When you restart the lab, the drive groups will be randomized. If you exit and restart the lab, the correct group might be in a different position.

Group #	Connection Type	Capacity	RPMs	Avg. Seek Time	Internal or External
Group 1					
Group 2					
Group 3					
Group 4					
Group 5					

2. Drag the drive to the Workbench.

3. In the Workbench, click the **Back** button.

4. In the Shelf, click the **Cables** category and drag an appropriate cable connector to the port on the back of the hard drive. The other connector moves to Workbench Connections.

5. In Workbench Connections, drag the connector to the appropriate port on the back of the computer.

6. In the Shelf, drag a power plug to the power receptacle on the back of the hard drive.

7. In Workbench Connections, drag the power plug to the electrical outlet.

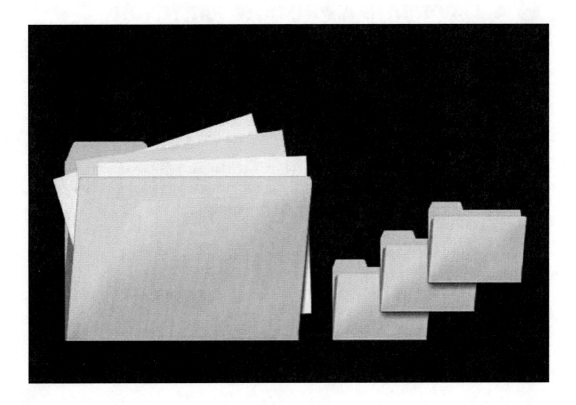

4.0

File System

4.1.4 CREATE A PRIMARY PARTITION

Scenario

You are preparing the hard disk configuration for a new Windows XP Professional computer. You want to create a second partition on the computer's hard disk. The new partition will store user data.

Your task in this lab is to create a new partition on Disk 0. The new partition should have the following properties:

- Type = Primary

- Size = 20000 MB

- Drive Letter = E

- File System = NTFS

- Name = Data

Steps

Before completing this lab, consider the following facts about basic disks. A basic disk is a physical disk type that can be accessed by all operating systems.

- A basic disk has a limit of four partitions, only one of which can be an extended partition.

- One primary partition must be marked active.

- A basic disk can only host basic volumes.

- Most operating systems can recognize only one primary partition. All other primary partitions are invisible. (Windows NT/2000/XP/Server 2003 can recognize multiple primary partitions.)

- The active primary partition is represented with one drive letter (C:). The extended partition can be divided into multiple logical drives (up to 26).

Complete the following steps:

1. Click **Start,** then right-click **My Computer** and select **Manage** to open the Computer Management console.

2. Select **Disk Management.** You should see a window similar to the one shown here.

3. Right-click unallocated space on Disk 0 and select **New Partition...** from the menu.

4. Click **Next** to start the New Partition Wizard. The following screen is shown.

5. Make sure **Primary partition** is selected and click **Next**. The following screen is shown.

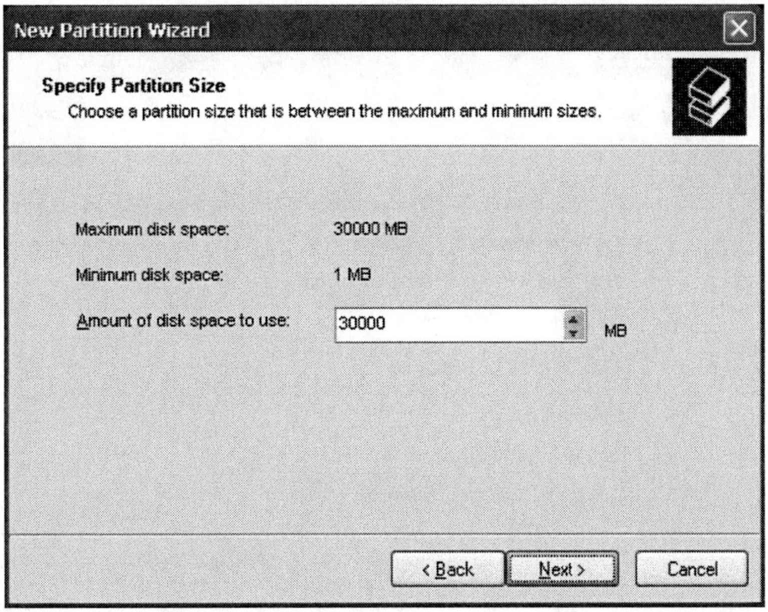

New Partition Wizard

Specify Partition Size
Choose a partition size that is between the maximum and minimum sizes.

Maximum disk space: 30000 MB

Minimum disk space: 1 MB

Amount of disk space to use: [30000] MB

[< Back]   [Next >]   [Cancel]

6. Type the amount of disk space required by the scenario, then click **Next**.

7. Make sure the drive letter required by the scenario is selected, then click **Next**. The following screen is shown.

New Partition Wizard

Format Partition
To store data on this partition, you must format it first.

Choose whether you want to format this partition, and if so, what settings you want to use.

○ Do not format this partition

◉ Format this partition with the following settings:

File system: NTFS

Allocation unit size: Default

Volume label: New Volume

☐ Perform a quick format

☐ Enable file and folder compression

< Back   Next >   Cancel

8. Enter the volume label required by the scenario.

9. Click **Finish** to create the partition.

4.1.5 CREATE A LOGICAL DRIVE

Scenario

You are preparing the hard disk configuration for a new Windows XP Professional computer. You want to create a new logical drive to store user data. You might create several such logical drives on this computer in the future.

Your task in this lab is to create a new extended partition that uses all the remaining space on Disk 0. Inside the extended partition, create a logical drive with the following properties:

- Type = Logical Drive

- Size = 5000 MB

- Drive Letter = E

- File System = NTFS

- Name = Data

Steps

In this scenario, you need to create a new *extended* partition on Disk 0 and create a *logical drive* within the partition.

As you complete this lab, notice the color coding that is shown in Disk Management for each of the disk partition types. Complete the following table throughout the lab.

Color	Disk object type
Dark Blue	
Black	
Light Green	
Dark Green	
Light Blue	

Complete the following steps:

1. Click **Start**, then right-click **My Computer** and select **Manage** to open Computer Management.

2. Select **Disk Management**.

3. Right-click unallocated space on the desired basic disk and select **New Partition....**

4. Click **Next** to start the New Partition Wizard. You are then prompted to select the partition type.

   Why is **Logical drive** disabled as an option?

   _____

5.   Select **Extended partition** and click **Next**.

6.   Accept all the remaining disk space for the partition. Click **Next**.

     Why weren't you prompted to define a drive letter and file system type?

     _____

7.   Click **Finish** to create the partition.

8.   Right-click free space in the desired extended partition and select **New Logical Drive...** from the menu.

9.   Click **Next** to start the New Partition Wizard.

     Why are the other partition types unavailable?

     _____

10. Click **Next**.

11. Type the amount of disk space to be used for the logical drive. Click **Next**.

12. Verify the drive letter and click **Next**.

13. Select the file system type and type the volume label. Click **Next**.

14. Click **Finish** to create the logical drive.

4.1.7 CREATE A SIMPLE VOLUME

Scenario

You have installed a new hard disk in your Windows XP system. You want to store video and music files on the disk, but you don't need all of the disk space. However, if you need to, you want to be able to increase the size of the volume without reformatting.

Your task in this lab is to create a new volume on Disk 2 with the following settings:

- Type=Simple

- Size=10 GB (10000 MB)

- Drive Letter=G

- File System=NTFS

- Volume Label=MultiMedia

Steps

Before completing this lab, consider the following facts about dynamic disks. A dynamic disk is a physical disk that can only be accessed by the Windows 2000/XP/Server 2003 operating systems. Other computers will not recognize volumes on a dynamic disk if the disk is imported into the system.

- Volumes on dynamic disks are like partitions and logical drives on basic disks.

- A volume can be made of non-contiguous space on a single drive or space taken from more than one drive.

- You cannot install the operating system on a dynamic disk. You can, however, upgrade a basic disk containing the operating system to dynamic after installation.

Complete the following steps:

1. Click **Start,** then right-click **My Computer** and select **Manage** to open the Computer Management console.

2. Select **Disk Management.**

3. Right-click Disk 2 at the left (be sure to select the disk rather than selecting a unit of storage on the disk) and select **Convert to Dynamic Disk...** from the menu. The following dialog opens.

4. Click **OK.**

   How did the description of Disk 2 change?

   _____

5. Once you convert the disk, you can create the new volume. Begin by right-clicking the unallocated space on the required disk and selecting **New Volume...** from the menu.

6. Click **Next** to start the New Volume wizard. The following screen is shown.

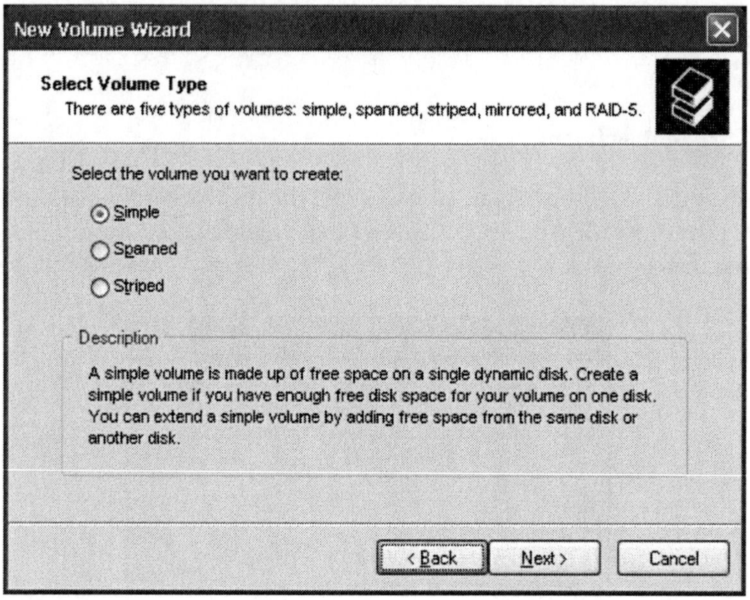

New Volume Wizard

Select Volume Type
There are five types of volumes: simple, spanned, striped, mirrored, and RAID-5.

Select the volume you want to create:

◉ Simple

○ Spanned

○ Striped

Description

A simple volume is made up of free space on a single dynamic disk. Create a simple volume if you have enough free disk space for your volume on one disk. You can extend a simple volume by adding free space from the same disk or another disk.

< Back   Next >   Cancel

7. Make sure the correct volume type is selected, then click **Next**. The following screen is shown.

```
New Volume Wizard                                             [X]

   Select Disks
      You can select the disks and set the disk size for this volume.

      Select the dynamic disk you want to use, and then click Add.
      Available:                                Selected:
      ┌─────────────────────┐                  ┌─────────────────────┐
      │ Disk 1      20000 MB│   [  Add >  ]    │ Disk 2      40000 MB│
      │                     │                  │                     │
      │                     │   [ < Remove  ]  │                     │
      │                     │                  │                     │
      │                     │   [ < Remove All]│                     │
      └─────────────────────┘                  └─────────────────────┘

                        Total volume size in megabytes (MB):        40000

      Maximum available space in MB:        40000

      Select the amount of space in MB:     40000   [▲▼]


                              [ < Back ] [  Next >  ] [ Cancel ]
```

8. In the **Select the amount of space in MB**, type the amount of disk space to be used for the new volume, then click **Next**.

9. Make sure the correct drive letter required by the scenario is selected, then click **Next**.

   What file system types are supported on simple volumes that are formatted through Disk Management?

   _____

10. Enter the volume label required by the scenario. Click **Next**.

11. Click **Finish** to create the partition.

4.2.5 FORMAT DRIVES

Scenario

You are a technician sent to set up a branch office computer. The branch office records financial data, stores it to disk (the **E:** drive), and transmits the information to the main office. After transmission, the reporting software automatically makes a daily backup of the transmission to floppy disk. Security requires you to make sure all systems run the NTFS file system.

Your task in this lab is to do the following:

- Format the diskette in drive **A:** (accept the default volume label).

- Format the **E:** drive with NTFS (use **branch2** for the volume label).

- Convert the **C:** drive from FAT32 to NTFS without losing the data already on the **C:** drive (use the current volume label **WINXP**).

Steps

You can format a disk or drive from the command line, Windows Explorer, or Disk Management. However, you must use the command line to convert a drive from FAT32 to NTFS.

Complete the following steps:

1. To format the floppy disk, click **Start**, then right-click **My Computer** and select **Explore** from the menu.

2. Right-click the **A:** drive and select **Format...** from the menu. The following dialog is shown.

3. Click **Start**, then click **OK** to confirm the format operation.

4. When the operation is complete, click **OK**.

5. Another way to format is using Disk Management. To do so, click the **Start** menu, then right-click **My Computer** and choose **Manage**.

6. Select **Disk Management**. The following screen is shown.

7. Right-click the **E:** volume and select **Format...** from the menu to open the dialog you see here.

8. Use **branch2** as the volume label and make sure the file system is NTFS. Click **OK**.

   What happens to existing data on the drive when you format it?

   _____

   What should you do prior to formatting a volume?

   _____

9. Click **OK** to confirm the action.

10. To convert the C: drive's file system to NTFS, you must use the command line. To open a command line, click **Start**, then select **Run....**

11. Type **cmd**, then click **OK**. A command line like the one below is shown.

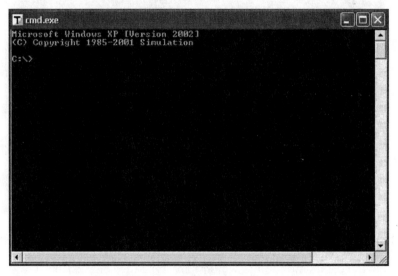

12. Type **convert /?** to see a list of options for the command.

    What does the **/V** switch do?

    _____

    What does the **/X** switch do?

    _____

13. Type **convert c: /fs:ntfs**. The following dialog is shown.

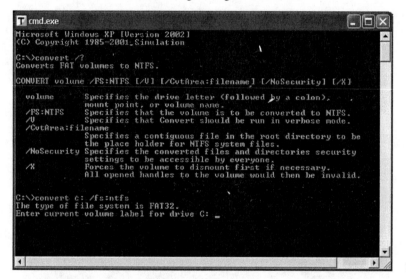

```
cmd.exe                                                          _ □ ×
Microsoft Windows XP [Version 2002]
(C) Copyright 1985-2001_Simulation
                                               \
C:\>convert /?
Converts FAT volumes to NTFS.

CONVERT volume /FS:NTFS [/V] [/CvtArea:filename] [/NoSecurity] [/X]

  volume         Specifies the drive letter (followed by a colon),
                 mount point, or volume name.
  /FS:NTFS       Specifies that the volume is to be converted to NTFS.
  /V             Specifies that Convert should be run in verbose mode.
  /CvtArea:filename
                 Specifies a contiguous file in the root directory to be
                 the place holder for NTFS system files.
  /NoSecurity    Specifies the converted files and directories security
                 settings to be accessible by everyone.
  /X             Forces the volume to dismount first if necessary.
                 All opened handles to the volume would then be invalid.


C:\>convert c: /fs:ntfs
The type of file system is FAT32.
Enter current volume label for drive C: _
```

14. You will be prompted to enter the volume label. To find the volume label, click **Start/My Computer**. The volume label will be listed before the drive letter (C:).

15. Return to the command prompt window and type the volume label. Press Enter.

4.3.4 USE COMMAND HELP

Click the **Lab** button and use the lab to answer the following questions.

- Which of the following commands compares the contents of two floppy diskettes?

- Which switch would you use with the COPY command to display the full filename while copying?

- Which switch available with the DIR command performs the same function as using | **more**?

Steps

To answer these questions, you will need to use **HELP** and /?.

Complete the following steps:

1. Click the **Lab** button to start.

2. Click **Start/Run....**

3. To open the command prompt, type **cmd** and click **OK**.

4. To view help for commands one screen at a time, type **help | more**.

   Which command compares the contents of two floppy disks?

   _____

5. Press the Space bar to move the output a screen at a time until you return to a command prompt.

6. Type **xcopy /?**.

    Which switch displays the full filename while copying?

    _____

7. Type **dir /?**.

    Which switch performs the same function as using | **more**?

    _____

4.3.5 MANAGE DIRECTORIES

Scenario

You are working at the command line performing disk maintenance. You want to move recovered files into a new directory, and you want to remove an old archive folder that was put on the computer by mistake.

Your task in this lab is to do the following:

- Create the **d:\utilities\recover** directory.

- Remove the **d:\software\arch98** archive directory.

Steps

In this lab, use the **md** (make directory) and **rd** (remove directory) commands. Because the **d:\software\arch98** folder contains files, you must also use the **/s** switch to make the command work successfully.

Complete the following steps:

1. At the command prompt, type **dir.**

   Why don't you see the directory the scenario requires you to remove?

   _____

2. Type the following command:

   md d:\utilities\recover

3. Verify that the directory exists by typing **dir d:\utilities.**

   What is in the **utilities** directory?

   _____

4. Type **d:**.

    How does the command prompt change affect the way you enter commands executed on the D: drive?

    _____

5. Type the following command:

    rd software\arch98 /s

6. Verify that the directory was deleted by typing **dir software**.

    What is in the software directory?

    _____

4.3.6 COPY FILES

Scenario

You are working at the command line. You want to copy files and directories from the D: drive to the C: drive. Your task in this lab is to copy the following to **c:\tools:**

- The **d:\cmdstrt.ini** and **d:\apconf.exe** files.

- The contents of the **d:\resources** directory.

Steps

In this lab, use the **copy** and **xcopy** commands to copy directories, subdirectories, and files at the command line. You can only copy directory contents with the **xcopy** command. To copy subdirectories, include the **/S** switch.

Complete the following steps:

1. Verify that the files you need to copy exist on the D: drive by typing **dir d:**.

    What are the sizes of the files?

    _____

2. Verify the contents of the c:\tools directory by typing **dir tools**.

    What is the current contents of the tools directory?

    _____

3. To copy the **apconf.exe** file, type the following command:

    copy d:\apconf.exe c:\tools

4. Copy the **cmdstrt.ini** file using the same command and syntax, that is

    command source destination

5. Verify that the files now exist in the tools directory using the **dir tools** command.

6. Try to copy the contents of the **d:\resources** directory by typing the following:

    xcopy d:\resources c:\tools

    What is the result of the command?

    _____

7. Verify that you copied the entire contents of the **d:\resources** directory by typing **dir d:\ resources.**

    What was not copied during the execution of the **xcopy** command?

    _____

8. Now copy the entire contents of **d:\resources** using the following command:

    xcopy d:\resources c:\tools /S

    (**Hint:** Type y then press Enter to overwrite the files.)

9. Type **dir tools.**

    How did using the **/s** switch affect the contents of the tools directory?

    _____

4.4.4 HIDE FILES

Scenario

You are working at the command line doing file maintenance. While you're at the command line, you want to hide some files.

Your task in this lab is to set the hidden file attribute on the following files:

- **d:\apconf.exe**
- **d:\cmdstrt.cfg**
- **d:\strt.bat**

Steps

In this lab, use the **attrib** command to mark files as hidden.

Complete the following steps:

1. To verify that the files exist on the D: drive, type **dir d:**.

2. To set the Hidden file attribute for the **strt.bat** file, type the following:

   attrib +H d:\strt.bat

3. Verify that the command worked by repeating step 1.

   What change to the **strt.bat** file lets you know that the command worked?

   _____

4. To set the Hidden file attribute for the other files in the scenario, repeat step 2 using the appropriate file names in the commands.

4.4.5 PROTECT FILES

Scenario

You have two application files that hold system parameters that you don't want to be modified. Working at the command line, you want to make these files read only.

Your task in this lab is to set the read only attribute on the following files:

- **c:\softcfg.cfg**
- **c:\pixel.cfg**

Steps

Complete the following steps:

1. Verify that the files exist by typing **dir**.

2. To set the Read only attribute on the file, type the following:

   attrib +R c:\softcfg.cfg

   attrib +R c:\pixel.cfg

4.5.3 USE DISK CLEANUP

Scenario

You want to free up space on the C: drive. Run Disk Cleanup and delete all extra files on the **C:** drive *except* Office Setup Files and files in the Recycle Bin. Do not compress old files.

Steps

Complete the following steps:

1. Click **Start**, then right-click **My Computer** and select **Explore** from the shortcut menu.

2. Right-click the **C:** drive and choose **Properties** from the shortcut menu. The following dialog is shown.

3. Click the **Disk Cleanup...** button to open the following dialog.

4. Select and read the descriptions for **Temporary Internet Files** and **Temporary Files.**

   What is the difference between the two?

   _____

   When can you safely delete files in the Temp directory?

   _____

5. Select and read the description for **Offline Web Pages.**

   How can you view your favorite Web pages offline after you've cleaned out these files?

   _____

6. Select the following types of files for deletion:
   ◦ Downloaded Program Files
   ◦ Temporary Internet Files
   ◦ Temporary Files

7. Deselect the following:
   ◦ Office Setup Files
   ◦ Recycle Bin
   ◦ Compress old files

8. Click **OK.**

9. Click **Yes** to confirm the cleanup.

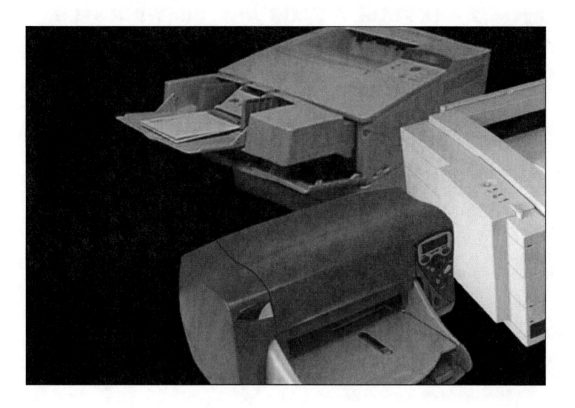

5.0

Printing

5.2.4 INSTALL A PLUG AND PLAY PRINTER

Scenario

You are configuring the printing environment for a Windows XP Professional computer. You have attached a parallel print device to the computer's LPT1 port and turned the print device on. The print device is Plug and Play compatible.

Your task in this lab is to add a local printer for the print device. Accept the default settings. You do not need to print a test page.

Steps

In this scenario, you need to create a new local printer. Do this by autodetecting the printer and accepting the default settings.

Complete the following steps:

1. Click **Start/Printers and Faxes**.

2. Select the **Add a printer** task in the Printer Tasks list.

    How should you install a printer connected to a USB port?

    _____

3. Click **Next** to begin the Add Printer wizard.

4. The **Local printer attached to this computer** option is selected by default. Also notice the **Automatically detect and install my Plug and Play printer** option is enabled. Click **Next**. Windows should detect the print device and install an appropriate driver.

5. Select **No** to skip printing a test page, then click **Next**.

6. Click **Finish**.

5.2.5 MANUALLY INSTALL A PRINTER

Scenario

You are configuring the printing environment for a Windows XP Professional computer. You have purchased the print device, but it has not yet arrived. The user will connect the print device to the local printer port after it arrives. Meanwhile, the user wants to send some print jobs to the printer's print queue. The user will pause the print queue and unpause it after connecting the print device.

Your task in this lab is to manually add a local printer using the following properties:

- Port = LPT1

- Manufacturer = HP

- Model= HP LaserJet 5Si

- Name = Dev-Prn2

- Shared = No

You do not need to print a test page.

Steps

Complete the following steps:

1. Click **Start,** then click **Printers and Faxes.**

2. In the **Printer Tasks** list, select the **Add a printer** task.

3. Click **Next** to begin the Add Printer wizard.

4. Clear the **Automatically detect and install my Plug and Play printer** option, then click **Next**. The following dialog is shown:

5. Select the printer port. Click **Next**.

6. Select the printer manufacturer and the model from the corresponding lists. Click **Next**.

7. Type the printer name and click **Next**.

8. Accept the default sharing behavior and click **Next**.

9. Select whether to print a test page (in the lab, printing a test page has no effect). Click **Next**.

10. Click **Finish** to complete the Add Printer wizard.

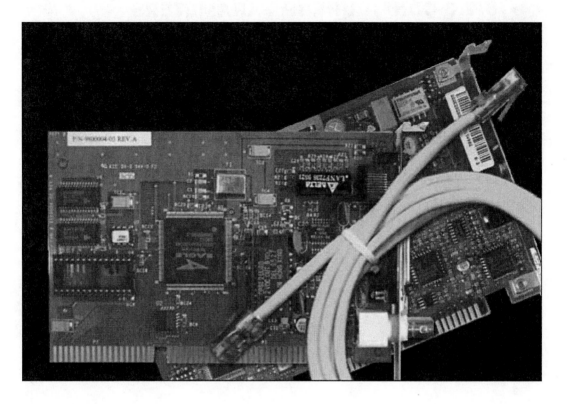

6.0
Networking

6.2.6 CONFIGURE IP PARAMETERS

Scenario

You have just purchased a new computer and need to connect it to a small business network. The network uses static addressing. Configure the TCP/IP settings as follows:

- IP address = 10.1.1.12

- Subnet mask = 255.255.255.0 (**Note:** This is *not* the default subnet mask.)

- Default gateway = 10.1.1.254

- DNS server addresses = 10.1.1.1, 10.1.1.2 (use this order)

Steps

Complete the following steps:

1. Click **Start/Control Panel.**

2. Select **Switch to Classic View.**

3. Double-click **Network Connections.**

4. Right-click the applicable network connection and select **Properties** to open the
    following dialog box.

5. Select **Internet Protocol (TCP/IP)** from the list of items used by the connection. Click the **Properties** button to open the following dialog box.

6. Select **Use the following IP address** and configure the values as given in the scenario.

   What happens when you move the cursor to the subnet mask field?

   _____

   Why is this value used?

   _____

7. Click **OK**.

8. Click **OK** again to close the properties of the network connection.

6.2.7 CONFIGURE A CLIENT FOR DHCP

Scenario

You are configuring network connections for a Windows Server 2003 computer. Previously, your network did not have a DHCP server, but you have just installed and configured one.

Your task in this lab is to configure the TCP/IP protocol for the Local Area Connection network connection to get IP addressing and DNS server information from the DHCP server.

Steps

Complete the following steps:

1. Click **Start/Control Panel**.

2. Double-click **Network Connections**.

3. Right-click **Local Area Connection** and choose **Properties**.

4. Select **Internet Protocol (TCP/IP)** and click the **Properties** button.

5. Make the following changes:

   - Select **Obtain an IP address automatically**. This option will use a DHCP server if one exists. Otherwise, it will use Automatic Private IP Addressing (APIPA) to assign an address between 169.254.0.0 and 169.254.255.255.
   - Select **Obtain DNS server address automatically** to obtain DNS server addresses from a DHCP server

   Click **OK** to save the changes.

6. Click **OK** again to close the properties of the network connection.

6.3.5 INSTALL THE MS NOVELL CLIENT

Scenario

You are configuring a Windows XP Professional computer to access a Novell NetWare server. You decide to use the NetWare client software supplied with Windows until you can obtain a copy of the Novell client software.

Your task in this lab is to install the Client Service for NetWare client software.

Steps

Complete the following steps.

1. Click **Start/Control Panel**.

2. Click **Switch to Classic View**.

3. Double-click **Network Connections**.

4. Right-click **Local Area Connection** and select **Properties**.

    What components are currently installed?

    _____

    _____

    _____

5. Click the **Install...** button. The following dialog is shown.

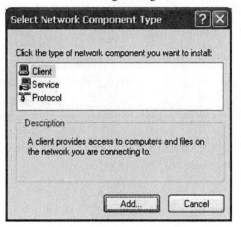

6. Verify that **Client** is selected, then click **Add....**

7. Accept the component to install, then click **OK.**

    What would you do to complete the process on a real system?

    _____

8. Click **OK** to close the message.

9. Right-click the network connection and select **Properties.**

    Which components were added when you installed the client component?

    _____

    _____

    _____

10. Click **Cancel.**

6.4.5 SHARE A FOLDER

Scenario

You are configuring the file system of a Windows XP Professional computer. The D:\Projects folder needs to be accessed by other users on the network. You have already configured appropriate NTFS permissions for the folder. Now you want to share the folder.

Your task in this lab is to share the D:\Projects folder using the share name *Projects*. Keep the default share permissions and other settings.

Steps

Complete the following steps:

1. Click **Start/My Computer.**

2. Navigate to the folder you want to share.

3. Right-click the folder and select **Sharing and Security....** The following dialog is shown.

4. Select **Share this folder**. Click **OK** to accept the default settings.

   How did the folder icon change?

   _____

6.4.7 MAP A DRIVE

Scenario

You are configuring the file system of a Windows XP Professional computer. You want to map a drive on this computer to a shared folder on the network.

Your task in this lab is to map the N: drive to the Projects shared folder on the NY-DEV-WRK3 computer. (The NY-DEV-WRK3 computer is part of the westsim.com domain.) Make sure the drive mapping is persistent, so you do not need to establish the drive mapping manually every time you log on.

Steps

Complete the following steps:

1. Click **Start/My Computer.**

2. From the **Tools** menu, select **Map Network Drive.** The following dialog is shown.

3. Select the drive letter from the **Drive** list. To select the network shared folder, click the **Browse...** button.

4. Expand the **westsim.com** domain and the **NY-DEV-WRK3** computer.

5. Select the **Projects** folder and click **OK.**

6. Select **Reconnect at logon** to restore the drive mapping each time you log on. Click **Finish.**

   How does the mapped drive icon differ from a physical drive icon?

6.5.4 SHARE A LOCAL PRINTER

Scenario

You are configuring the printing environment for a Windows XP Professional computer. You want to let other users on the network print to a local printer on the computer.

Your task in this lab is to share the Local LPT1 printer on this computer. Use a share name of Dev-Prn2 and make sure the printer is published to Active Directory.

Steps

Complete the following steps:

1. Click **Start/Printers and Faxes**.

2. Right-click the printer you want to share and select **Sharing...** from the menu. The following dialog is shown.

3. Select **Share this printer** and type the share name.

   What should you do if the printer is shared with computers that run different operating system versions?

   _____

4. Click **OK** to share the printer.

   How did the printer icon change?

   _____

6.5.5 ADD A NETWORK PRINTER

Scenario

You are configuring the printing environment for a Windows XP Professional computer. You want the workstation to be able to print to a network printer.

Your task in this lab is to use the Add Printer wizard to connect to the Dev-Prn1 printer on the NY-DEV-SRV1 network server.

Steps

Complete the following steps:

1. Click **Start/Printers and Faxes**.

2. In the Printer Tasks list, select the **Add a printer** task.

3. Click **Next** to begin the Add Printer wizard.

4. Select **A network printer, or a printer attached to another computer**. Click **Next**.

5. In the **Name** box, type the UNC path to the printer share. A UNC path uses the format *server_name**share_name*. Click **Next**.

6. Click **Finish**.

    How can you tell the difference between a network printer and a local printer?

    _____

6.6.4 CREATE A WIRELESS CONNECTION

Scenario

You have to issue a new laptop to an employee. Before you do, you want to configure a connection to your company's wireless network.

Your task in this lab is to create a new wireless connection as follows:

- Use **OurCompany** for the SSID.

- Use WEP encryption.

- Define **12345abcde** as the WEP key.

- Do not save settings to a flash drive.

Steps

You can configure a wireless network connection using the Wireless Network Setup Wizard.

Complete the following steps:

1. Click **Start/Control Panel**.

2. Select **Switch to Classic View**.

3. Double-click the **Wireless Network Setup Wizard** applet.

4. Click **Next** to begin the wizard. The following wizard screen is shown.

5. Type the SSID (Service Set Identification) in the **Network Name (SSID):** text box, and select **Manually assign a network key**.

6. Click **Next** to open the wizard screen shown here.

```
┌────────────────────────────────────────────────────────────────┐
│ Wireless Network Setup Wizard                               [X]  │
├────────────────────────────────────────────────────────────────┤
│   Enter a WEP key for your wireless network.                     │
│                                                                  │
├──────────────────────────────────────────────────────────────── │
│   The WEP (or Wired Equivalent Privacy) key must meet one of the │
│   following guidelines:                                          │
│   - Exactly 5 or 13 characters                                   │
│   - Exactly 10 or 26 characters using 0-9 and A-F                │
│   A longer WEP key is more secure than a short one.              │
│                                                                  │
│                                                                  │
│       Network key:       [***********************]  [26 characters] │
│       Confirm network key: [***********************] [26 characters] │
│                          ☑ Hide characters as I type             │
│                                                                  │
│   On the last page of this wizard, you can print this key and your│
│   other network settings for safekeeping.                        │
│                                                                  │
│                              < Back   [ Next > ]    Cancel       │
└────────────────────────────────────────────────────────────────┘
```

What are the requirements for the WEP key?

_____

7. Enter the key in the **Network key:** text box, then re-enter the key in the **Confirm network key:** text box. (**Tip:** If you have problems entering the key, deselect the **Hide characters as I type** check box, then enter and re-enter the key.) Click **Next**. The following wizard screen is shown.

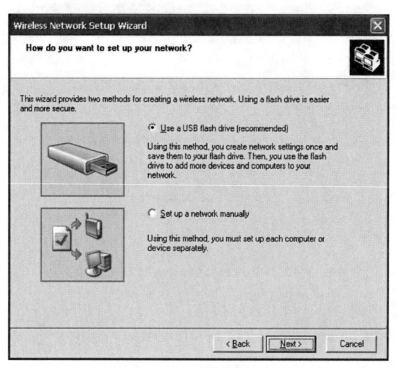

8. Choose the option that allows you to set up each device separately on the network, then click **Next**.

9. Click **Finish**.

10. To view the connection, click **Start**, right-click **My Network Places,** and choose **Properties.**

11. Right-click **Wireless Network Connection** and select **Properties.**

12. Click the **Wireless Network** tab. The following dialog is shown.

13. Select the **OurCompany** network, then click the **Properties** button.

    What is the value for the network authentication setting?

    _____

    What is the value for the data encryption setting?

    _____

14. Click **Cancel.**

6.6.7 USE WPA ENCRYPTION

Scenario

To increase the security of your wireless network, you have decided to use WPA instead of WEP. You need to define a wireless connection using WPA.

Your task in this lab is to create a new wireless connection as follows:

- Use **OurCompany** for the SSID.

- Use WPA encryption.

- Define **xyz123abc789** as the key.

- Do not save settings to a flash drive.

Steps

Complete the following steps:

1. Click **Start/Control Panel**.

2. Select **Switch to Classic View**.

3. Double-click the **Wireless Network Setup Wizard** apple.

4. Click **Next** to begin the wizard.

5. Type the SSID (Service Set Identification) in the **Network Name (SSID):** text box, and do the following:

    ○   Select the option that allows you to assign a key yourself.
    ○   Select the option that allows you to use WPA encryption.

    Click **Next**.

6. Enter the key in the **Network key:** text box, then re-enter the key in the **Confirm network key:** text box. (**Tip:** If you have problems entering the key, deselect the **Hide characters as I type** check box, then enter and re-enter the key.)

    What are the requirements for the WPA key?

    _____

7. Click **Next.**

8. Choose the option that allows you to set up each device separately on the network, then click **Next.**

9. Click **Finish.**

10. To view the connection, click **Start**, right-click **My Network Places**, and choose **Properties.**

11. Right-click **Wireless Network Connection** and select **Properties.**

12. Click the **Wireless Networks** tab.

13. Select the **OurCompany** network, then click the **Properties** button.

    What is the value for the network authentication setting?

    _____

    What is the value for the data encryption setting?

    _____

14. Click **Cancel.**

6.7.4 CREATE A DIALUP INTERNET CONNECTION

Scenario

You are configuring network connections for a Windows XP Professional computer. You want to create a dial-up connection to the Internet on this computer.

Your task in this lab is to use the New Connection wizard in Network Connections to create a dial-up Internet connection on this computer manually with the following properties:

- Connection Name/ISP Name = Dial Internet

- Phone Number = 555-1234

- User Name = wacky123

- Password = 56passgo

- Always use this user name and password? = True

- Default Internet connection? = True

- Firewalled? = True

Steps

Complete the following steps:

1. Click **Start**, then right-click **My Network Places** and select **Properties**.

2. In the **Network Connections** folder, select the **Create a new connection** network task.

3. Click **Next** to start the New Connection wizard.

    Which option would you choose to configure a parallel connection to another computer?

    _____

4. Verify that **Connect to the Internet** is selected, then click **Next**.

5. Select the option that allows you to configure the connection manually. Click **Next**.

6. Verify that you are using a modem. Click **Next**.

7. Type the ISP name and click **Next**.

8. Type the phone number and click **Next**.

9. Type the user name and password. Click **Next**.

10. Click **Finish** to create the connection.

6.8.3 FIND CONFIGURATION INFORMATION 1

Click the **Lab** button and use the lab to answer the following questions.

- What is the IP address of the workstation?

- How is the IP address configured on the system?

- Which DNS server will the computer contact if the first DNS server is unavailable?

Steps

To answer these questions, you can either view the TCP/IP properties of the network adapter, or use the **Ipconfig** command.

Complete the following steps:

1. Click the **Lab** button to start.

2. Click **Start/Run....**

3. To open the command prompt, type **cmd** and click **OK**.

4. Type **ipconfig** to view IP configuration information.

   What is the IP address of the workstation?

   _____

5. To see additional information about the TCP/IP configuration, type **ipconfig /all**.

   What is the value for **DHCP Enabled**? What does this indicate about how the IP address was obtained?

   _____

   _____

   What is the value for **DNS Servers**?

   _____

   Which DNS server will be used if the first one is unavailable?

   _____

6. Click the **Done** button and use the information from steps 4 and 5 to answer the questions.

6.8.4 FIND CONFIGURATION INFORMATION 2

Click the **Lab** button and use the lab to answer the following questions.

- What is the address of the DHCP server from which this workstation received it's IP configuration information?

- What is the default gateway address?

- What is the MAC address of the LAN adapter?

Steps

To answer these questions, you will need to use the **Ipconfig /all** command.

Complete the following steps:

1. Click the **Lab** button to start.

2. Click **Start/Run....**

3. To open the command prompt, type **cmd** and click **OK**.

4. Type **ipconfig /all** to view IP configuration information.

   What is the value for **DHCP Server**?

   _____

   What is the value for the **Default Gateway**?

   _____

   What is the value for the **Physical Address**?

   _____

5. Click the **Done** button and use the information from step 4 to answer the questions.

6.8.6 FIND PATH INFORMATION 1

Scenario

Click the **Lab** button to run the lab. Click the Wrk1 computer to open a DOS command line and identify the path between Wrk1 and Wrk3.

From the IP addresses listed below, list the addresses of the routers in the path between Wrk1 and Wrk3. Make sure each address is listed in order from top to bottom.

193.5.118.1	_____
193.5.118.2	_____
199.116.22.1	_____
205.10.12.1	_____
205.10.12.2	_____
209.53.182.1	_____
214.230.15.1	
214.230.15.2	
222.70.1.1	
222.70.1.2	

Explanation

Use the **tracert 215.61.199.2** command to trace the path between Wrk1 and Wrk3. The following routers are in the path (in this order):

1. 199.116.22.1

2. 214.230.15.2

3. 222.70.1.1

4. 205.10.12.2

You will also see the address 215.61.199.2 in the path, but this is Wrk3 and not a router in the path.

6.9.3 TROUBLESHOOT IP CONFIGURATION PROBLEMS

You are in charge of a small network as shown in the following graphic. The network is connected to the Internet and uses DHCP for address assignment.

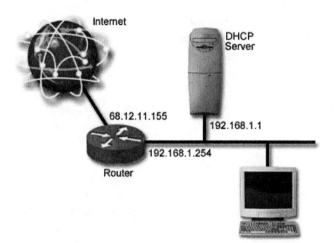

A user reports that his workstation can only communicate with some computers. Click the **Lab** button and use the **Ipconfig** command to diagnose the problem.

Based on the **Ipconfig** output, what is the most likely cause of the problem?

- ○ A. The DHCP server is down.
- ○ B. The DHCP server has been configured with the wrong default gateway address.
- ○ C. There is a rogue DHCP server on the network.
- ○ D. The default gateway and DNS server addresses have not been configured on the DHCP server.
- ○ E. The workstation has been configured to use static addressing.

Explanation

The correct answer is A.

To answer this question, run **Ipconfig /all** to get additional details about the system configuration.

You should notice the following problems:

- The default gateway and DNS server addresses have not been configured on the workstation. This means that communication is limited to other computers on the local network.

- The DHCP Enabled line is Yes, meaning that the workstation is configured to use a DHCP server.

- The DHCP Server address listed is blank. This means that the workstation was unable to contact the DHCP server.

- The IP address is in the APIPA range (169.254.0.1 to 169.254.255.254). This means that the workstation assigned itself an IP address. The workstation will be able to communicate with other hosts on the local network that have also configured their own IP address through APIPA.

Because the workstation could not contact a DHCP server, make sure the DHCP server is up and has a connection to the network.

6.9.4 TROUBLESHOOT NETWORK COMMUNICATION 1

Click the **Lab** button to run the lab. Use the **ping** and **tracert** commands from Wrk1 to diagnose the problem and answer the following question.

Wrk1 cannot communicate with Wrk3. Which of the following is the most likely cause of the problem?

   ◯ A. The switch is turned off.

   ◯ B. Wrk1 has been configured with an incorrect IP address or mask.

   ◯ C. The cable between Wrk3 and the switch needs to be replaced.

   ◯ D. Wrk3 has an incorrect default gateway setting.

   ◯ E. The IP address has not been configured on the switch.

Explanation

The correct answer is C.

Of the problems listed here, a bad cable between Wrk3 and the switch is the most likely cause of the problem.

To identify the problem, you can simply ping each workstation from Wrk1. You will find that Wrk1 can communicate with all hosts on the network except for Wrk3 (ping to Wrk2 and Wrk4 succeeds, but ping to Wrk3 fails). The problem appears to be isolated to Wrk3.

Other possible problems (not listed in the question) might include:

- The switch port to Wrk3 has been disabled.

- Wrk3 is configured with an IP address that is not on the same network.

- Wrk3 is down.

Because Wrk1 can communicate with Wrk2 and Wrk4, you know the following:

- Wrk1 has been configured with an IP address and mask compatible with the other hosts on the network.

- The switch is on. At least the three ports connecting Wrk1, Wrk2, and Wrk4 are operational.

Because this scenario involves devices on the same network, the default gateway setting on any host is not needed. In addition, the switch does not require an IP address in order to switch traffic between hosts on the network.

6.9.5 TROUBLESHOOT NETWORK COMMUNICATION 2

Click the **Lab** button to run the lab. Use the **ping** and **tracert** commands from Wrk1 and Wrk2 to diagnose the problem and answer the following question.

Wrk1 cannot communicate with Wrk3. Which of the following is the most likely cause of the problem?

○ A. Wrk1 has an incorrect default gateway setting.

○ B. The router is down.

○ C. The cable between Wrk1 and the switch needs to be replaced.

○ D. The cable between Wrk3 and the switch needs to be replaced.

○ E. Wrk1 has been configured with an incorrect IP address or mask.

Explanation

The correct answer is A.

Of the problems listed here, a missing or incorrect default gateway setting on Wrk1 is the most likely cause of the problem.

One way to troubleshoot the problem is as follows:

1. From Wrk1, ping Wrk3. You will see that the ping fails.

2. From Wrk1, ping another host on the remote network (such as Wrk4). You will find that ping to this device fails as well. At this point, you might start to assume that Wrk1 cannot communicate with any host on the remote network.

3. From Wrk1, ping a host on the same network as Wrk1 (such as Wrk2). You will find that this succeeds. You now know that Wrk1 can communicate with at least one host on the local network, but likely cannot communicate with any hosts on the remote network. This means that Wrk1 has a good connection to the switch and that the IP address and mask on Wrk1 have been configured correctly.

4. Test connectivity to the router by pinging the local router interface (192.168.1.1) from Wrk1. You will find that this ping succeeds. This means the router is up and accessible.

5. If you want, you can ping the remote router interface (192.168.2.1) from Wrk1. You will find that Wrk1 cannot communicate with this remote router interface. This means that packets from Wrk1 to the remote network cannot even make it through the router.

6. From Wrk2, ping Wrk3. You will find that this succeeds. That means that the communication problem is likely isolated to Wrk1. You know that the router has a good connection to the remote network.

At this point, you know that:

• Wrk1 can communicate with local hosts

• Wrk1 cannot communicate with hosts on the other network.

• Wrk2 can communicate with hosts on the other network.

It appears that the problem is isolated to Wrk1. This means that it has an incorrect or missing default gateway setting.

6.9.6 TROUBLESHOOT NETWORK COMMUNICATION 3

Click the **Lab** button to run the lab. Use the **ping** and **tracert** commands from Wrk1 and Wrk2 to diagnose the problem and answer the following question.

Wrk1 cannot communicate with Wrk3. Which of the following are the most likely causes of the problem? (Select all that apply.)

❏   A.   Wrk1 has an incorrect default gateway setting.

❏   B.   Switch2 does not have an IP address configured.

❏   C.   The cable between Wrk3 and the switch needs to be replaced.

❏   D.   Switch2 is down.

❏   E.   Wrk3 has an incorrect subnet mask setting.

❏   F.   Wrk3 had an incorrect default gateway setting.

Explanation

The correct answers are C, E, and F.

Of the problems listed here, the following might be causing the communication problem:

- The cable between Wrk3 and the switch needs to be replaced.

- Wrk3 had an incorrect default gateway setting.

- Wrk3 has an incorrect subnet mask setting.

Following is one way to troubleshoot this problem:

1. From Wrk1, ping Wrk3 to verify the problem. The ping test fails.

2. From Wrk1, ping another host on the remote network (such as Wrk4). You will find that this test succeeds.

Because Wrk1 can communicate with another host on the remote network, you know that:

- Wrk1 is correctly configured with a default gateway address.

- The connection between Wrk1 and the remote network is valid.

- Switch2 is up (messages can go through the switch to Wrk4).

- The problem is likely isolated to Wrk3. Therefore, additional troubleshooting should take place at or around Wrk3.

Remember, switches do not need an IP address configured to be able to perform switching functions.

8.0
Security

8.1.4 CONFIGURE NTFS PERMISSIONS 1

Scenario

You have been asked to perform administrative tasks for a computer that is not a member of a domain. There are two groups of users who access the computer: Day Group and Night Group. Each group has a corresponding folder: **D:\Day Data** and **D:\Night Data**, respectively.

Your task in this lab is to:

- Turn off permissions inheritance for D:\Day Data and D:\Night Data.

- Remove the Users group from the ACL of each folder.

- Add the appropriate group to the folder ACL.

- Assign Full Control over each folder to the appropriate group.

- Do not change any other permissions assigned to other users or groups.

Steps

Complete the following tasks:

1. To set NTFS permissions for the D:\Day Data folder, click **Start** then **My Computer.**

2. Double-click the **D:** drive, then right-click the **Day Data** folder and select **Properties.**

3. Click the **Security** tab. The following dialog is shown.

Selecting a user or a group in the top box displays the NTFS permissions in the bottom box. What NTFS permissions have been assigned to the following objects?

Group	NTFS Permissions
Administrators	
Creator Owner	
System	
Users	

4. Try to remove the **Users** group by selecting it in the Group or user names window, then clicking **Remove**.

    What prevents you from deleting the group?

    _____

5. To turn off permissions inheritance, click the **Advanced** button. The following dialog is shown.

6. Deselect **Allow inheritable permissions from parent to propagate to this object and all child objects. Include these with entries explicitly defined here.** The following dialog is shown.

```
┌─────────────────────────────────────────────────────────────┐
│ Security                                                  [X] │
├─────────────────────────────────────────────────────────────┤
│        Selecting this option means that the parent permission │
│  (?)   entries that apply to child objects will not longer be │
│        applied to this object.                                │
│                                                               │
│        - To copy the permission entries that were previously  │
│        applied from the parent to this object, click Copy.    │
│        - To remove the permission entries that were previously│
│        applied from the parent and keep only those permissions│
│        explicitly defined here, click Remove.                 │
│        - To cancel this action, click Cancel.                 │
│                                                               │
│         [ Copy ]    [ Remove ]    [ Cancel ]                  │
└─────────────────────────────────────────────────────────────┘
```

What happens if you select the **Remove** option?

_____

7. Choose the option that retains the permissions inherited from the parent object, then click **OK.**

8. Try to remove the **Users** group again by selecting it and clicking **Remove.**

    How did the result differ this time?

    _____

    If you've chosen to retain the permissions on the folder, why were you still able to delete the Users group?

    _____

9. With permission inheritance turned off and the Users group removed, you can add the appropriate group to the ACL. To add a group click **Add....** The following dialog is shown.

10. Type **Day Group** in the object names window, then click **OK**.

11. Select **Day Group** in the Group or user names: window and select the permissions required by the scenario in the Permissions for Day Group window.

12. Click **OK**.

13. With the permissions configured for the Day Data folder, you can configure the permissions for the Night Data folder. Right-click the **Night Data** folder and select **Properties.**

14. Click the **Security** tab.

15. Click the **Advanced** button.

16. Deselect **Allow inheritable permissions from parent to propagate to this object and all child objects. Include these with entries explicitly defined here.**

17. Click **Copy,** then click **OK.**

18. Select **Users** and click **Remove.**

19. Click the **Add...** button.

20. Type **Night Group** in the object names window, then click **OK.**

21. Select **Night Group** in the Group or user names: window and select the permissions required by the scenario in the Permissions for Day Group window.

22. Click **OK.**

8.1.5 CONFIGURE NTFS PERMISSIONS 2

Scenario

You are configuring NTFS permissions on a computer that is not a domain member. You are working on the **D:\Projects** folder. Your task in this lab is to:

- Turn off permissions inheritance for D:\Projects.

- Remove the Users group from the ACL.

- Add the **mlewis** user and allow the user to do everything except assign permissions.

- Add the **krhodes** user and allow the user to look at but not change files.

- Leave all other permissions intact.

Steps

The **Security** tab lists each security principal (user, computer, or group) who has permission to the drive, folder, or file. The following permissions are available:

- **Full Control.** Lets the security principal perform all actions to the object, including changing permissions and taking ownership of the object.

- **Modify.** Same as **Read & Execute**, **List Folder Contents**, **Read**, and **Write** permissions plus lets the security principal delete the object.

- **Read & Execute.** Same as the **Read** permission plus lets the security principal traverse folders and execute files.

- **List Folder Contents.** (Folders Only) Same as the **Read & Execute** permission, but the permission is only inherited by folders.

- **Read.** Lets the security principal read the object's data and other attributes, including listing a folder's contents.

- **Write.** Lets the security principal change the object's data and other attributes, including creating files and folders within a folder.

Complete the following steps:

1. Begin modifying the NTFS permissions for the folder by clicking **Start/My Computer**.

2. Open the **D:** drive, then right-click the **Projects** folder and select **Properties**.

3. Select the **Security** tab, then click the **Advanced** button.

4. To turn off permissions inheritance, deselect **Allow inheritable permissions from the parent to propagate to this object and all child objects. Include these with entries explicitly defined here.**

5. Click **Copy**, then click **OK**.

6. Remove the **Users** group by selecting it, then clicking the **Remove** button.

7. To add a user click **Add....**

8. Type **mlewis** and click **OK**.

9. Select **mlewis** in the list, then deselect all the permissions listed. After you have removed all the permissions for **mlewis**, select the **Modify** permissions.

   Which permissions accompany Modify?

   _____

10. Assign **mlewis** the permissions required by the scenario.

11. Repeat steps 7 through 10 to add the **krhodes** user.

12. Select **krhodes** and assign the required permissions.

13. Click **OK**.

8.1.7 CONFIGURE SHARED FOLDER PERMISSIONS

Scenario

You are configuring the file system of a Windows XP Professional computer. The D:\Projects folder is located on a FAT32 partition and has been shared using the share name Projects. You want to make sure that only users of the Research local group can read, write, and delete this shared folder's contents.

Your task in this lab is to configure share permissions for the Projects shared folder so that only members of the Research local group can view, change, and delete its contents. To do this, take the following actions:

1. In Explorer, edit the properties of the D:\Projects folder.

2. On the Sharing tab, click the **Permissions** button.

3. Remove Everyone from the permission list.

4. Add the Research local group.

5. Grant the group Allow Full Control permissions to the share.

Steps

Complete the following steps:

1. Click **Start/My Computer.**

2. Double-click the **D:** drive, then right-click the **Projects** folder and select **Sharing and Security....**

3. Click the **Permissions** button. The following dialog is shown.

4. To remove the **Everyone** group, click the **Remove** button.

5. Click **Add.**

6. Type **Research**, then click **OK.**

7. Select the **Research** group and configure the permissions required by the scenario.

8. Click **OK**, then click **OK** again to exit the Project Permissions dialog box.

8.1.9 CONFIGURE PRINTER PERMISSIONS

Scenario

You are configuring the printing environment for a Windows XP Professional computer. This computer has two printers named Dev-Prn2 and Dev-Prn3. Each printer prints to a separate print device. You want to let everyone on the network print to the Dev-Prn2 printer, but you only want to let users who are members of the Research local group print to the Dev-Prn3 printer.

Your task in this lab is to configure permissions for the Dev-Prn3 printer so that only the Research local group can print to the printer. When you are done, the Administrators group and the Power Users group should still be able to manage printers and documents. Take the following actions:

1. Edit the properties of the Dev-Prn3 printer.

2. On the Security tab, remove Everyone from the ACL.

3. Add the Research local group to the ACL.

4. Grant the Research domain group the Print permission.

5. Do not change the permissions for CREATOR OWNER, Administrators and Power Users. **Note:** You cannot prevent Administrators and Power Users from being able to print to the printer while still allowing them to manage the printer and its documents.

Steps

Complete the following steps:

1. Click **Start/Printers and Faxes**.

2. Right-click the **Dev-Prn3** printer and select **Properties**.

3. Select the **Security** tab. The following dialog opens.

4. Select the **Everyone** group, then click **Remove**.

5. To add the Research group, click the **Add** button.

6. Type **Research**, then click **OK**.

7. Click **OK** to apply the changes and exit.

8.2.3 CONFIGURE POLICIES

Scenario

You have decided to implement additional security for a specific workstation. Make the following changes to the Local Security Policy:

- Remove the Users group from the list of those authorized to shut down the system.

- Restrict CD-ROM access to locally logged-on users.

- Hide the last username at logon.

Steps

Complete the following steps:

1. To open the Local Security Policy editor, select **Start/Administrative Tools/Local Security Policy**. The following dialog is shown.

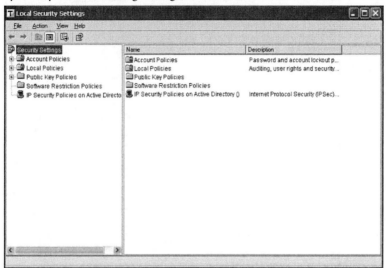

2.   Expand **Local Policies** and select **User Rights Assignment**.

3.   In the right window, right-click **Shut down the system** and select **Properties** from the menu. The following dialog is shown.

4.   Select the group the scenario requires you to remove and click the **Remove** button.

5.   Click **OK**.

6.   To edit the final two policies, select the **Security Options** folder.

7. Right-click **Devices: Restrict CD-ROM access to locally logged-on user only** and select **Properties.** The dialog is similar to the one shown here.

8. Select **Enabled,** then click **OK.**

9. Right-click **Interactive logon: Do not display last user name in logon screen** and select **Properties.**

10. Select **Enabled,** then click **OK.**

8.2.5 ENFORCE PASSWORD SETTINGS

Scenario

You are the administrator for a small non-domain network. You want to improve the password security of your own Windows XP Professional workstation. Use the Local Security Policy tool and configure the following password restrictions:

- Passwords must be 8 characters

- Passwords must be changed every 30 days

- Passwords must contain non-alphabetical characters

Note: Policy changes will not be enforced within the lab.

Steps

Complete the following table with the necessary settings for this scenario.

Password Policy	Setting
Minimum password length	
Maximum password age	
Password must meet complexity requirements	

Complete the following steps:

1. Click **Start/Administrative Tools/Local Security Policy.**

2. In the Local Security Policy editor, browse to **Account Policies/Password Policy.**

3. In the right window, right-click the policy you want to edit and select **Properties.**

4. Configure the policy settings and click **OK.**

5. Repeat steps 3 and 4 to configure additional policies.

    What is the difference between the minimum password age and the maximum password age?

    _____

    Which setting would you configure to prevent users from re-using previous passwords?

    _____

8.3.3 ENABLE AUDITING

Scenario

You have a computer that is shared between multiple users in your dorm room. Recently, you have noticed that the system clock keeps getting reset. You are also concerned that someone might be logging in with your username and password while you aren't around, either at the console or remotely.

Your task in this lab is to configure auditing as follows:

- Enable auditing for successful privilege use events. This will log an event each time the system clock is changed.

- Enable auditing for both successful and failed logon events. This will log an event each time someone tries or is able to log on using an account.

Note: In both cases, you will likely capture more events than you really want. You will have to look through the Security event log to distinguish between changing the system time from other privilege use events and to identify the user account that was used for logon events.

Steps

Complete the following steps:

1. Select **Start/Administrative Tools/Local Security Policy**.

2. Expand **Local Policies**, then select **Audit Policy**.

3. Double-click the **Audit privilege use** policy. The following window is shown.

4. Configure the policy to detect successful privilege use events, then click **OK**.

5. Double-click the **Audit logon events** policy.

6. Configure the policy to detect successful and unsuccessful logon events, then click **OK**.

8.4.4 CONFIGURE THE WINDOWS FIREWALL

Scenario

A security audit showed that a number of computers are not running the Windows firewall. You are working on correcting the problem on the current system. Your task in this lab is to do the following:

- Enable the Windows firewall.

- Allow Remote Desktop and Remote Assistance through the firewall.

Steps

You can configure the Windows firewall settings through the Control Panel.

Complete the following steps:

1. Click **Start/Control Panel**.

2. Select **Switch to Classic View**.

3. Double-click the **Windows Firewall** applet. The following dialog is shown.

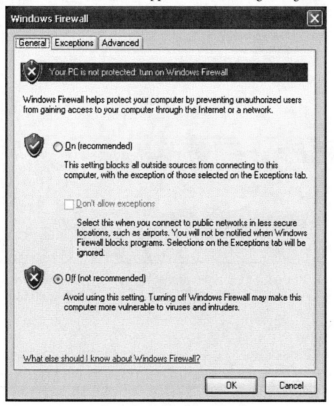

4. Under the General tab, select **On** to enable the firewall.

5. To allow specific kinds of network traffic, click the **Exceptions** tab. The following dialog is shown.

6. Select the check boxes for the types of traffic you wish to allow. (You can also deselect check boxes for the types of allowed traffic that you do not want to permit.)

7. Click the **General** tab.

    How would the **Don't allow exceptions** option affect the exceptions you have just defined?

    _____

8. Click **OK**.

8.5.3 ADD A TRUSTED SITE

Scenario

You work for a biotech research firm and are trying to access a new internal web server called acct. westsim.private. After logging on, you see a warning message that instructs you to add the site to your trusted site list.

Your task in this lab is to use Internet Options in the Control Panel to add the acct.westsim. private URL to the Trusted sites zone in Internet Explorer. The site does *not* support SSL (https). In the lab, precede the URL with either *http://* or *https://* as appropriate.

Note: To open the Internet Options applet, use the Classic View in the Control Panel.

Steps

Complete the following steps:

1.   Click **Start/Control Panel.**

2.   Select **Network and Internet Connections.**

3.   Select **Internet Options.**

4.   Click the **Security** tab. The following dialog is shown.

5. Select the **Trusted Sites** zone, then click the **Sites...** button. The following dialog is shown.

6. Deselect the **Require server verification (https:) for all sites in this zone** option, then type the URL for the Web site. Use the following syntax for the URL: *http://acct.westsim. private*. Click **Add**.

7. Click **OK**.

8. Click **OK** to close the Internet Options.

8.5.4 ADD A RESTRICTED SITE

Scenario

You administer a Windows XP Professional computer. Users of the computer must often go to the www.networkinghistory.com web site for reference information. However, they are inundated by popup advertisement screens when they surf that site. You discover that the popups for the site come from the following locations:

- http://www.myads.com

- http://www.badads.com

Disable popup ads by:

- Adding these two sites to the Restricted sites zone (be sure to precede each site with http://).

- Disabling Active scripting for the *Internet* zone (note that disabling this feature disables all scripts on the page).

Note: To open the Internet Options applet, use the Classic View in the Control Panel.

Steps

1. Click **Start/Control Panel.**

2. Click **Switch to Classic View.**

3. Double-click **Internet Options.**

4. Click the **Security** tab.

5. Select the **Restricted Sites** zone, then click the **Sites...** button.

6. Type the URL for the Web site. Use the following syntax for the URL: *http://www.myads.com.*

   Click **Add**. Repeat the process for any additional sites you want to add.

7. Click **OK**.

   Select each of the zones and note the default security level below.

Zone	Default Security Level
Internet	
Local intranet	
Trusted sites	
Restricted sites	

8. Select the **Internet** zone, then click the **Custom Level...** button.

   What is the default setting for the following options?

Option	Setting
Download signed ActiveX controls	
Download unsigned ActiveX controls	
File download	
Java permissions	
Launching programs and files in an IFRAME	

9. For the **Scripting/Active scripting** entry, select **Disable**. Click **OK**.

   What happened to the Internet zone security level?

   _____

10. Click **OK** to close the Internet Options.

8.5.5 CUSTOMIZE ZONE SETTINGS

Scenario

You work for a software company that, among other things, designs custom ActiveX controls. You have been assigned to one of the teams to help test the new software. To ensure that testing will not be impeded by the current security settings, you decide to change the security settings for Internet content for the Intranet zone.

Your task in this lab is to edit the Security for the Intranet zone as follows:

- Enable downloading of signed ActiveX controls

- Prompt when downloading unsigned ActiveX controls

- Configure the Microsoft virtual machine Java settings to use Low safety

Note: To open the Internet Options applet, use the Classic View in the Control Panel.

Steps

Complete the following table with the necessary settings to meet the scenario requirements.

Option	Setting
ActiveX controls and plug-ins\run ActiveX controls and plug-ins	
Microsoft VM\Java permissions	
Miscellaneous\Submit nonencrypted form data	

Complete the following steps:

1. Click **Start/Control Panel**.

2. Click **Switch to Classic View**.

3. Double-click **Internet Options**.

4. Click the **Security** tab.

5. Select the **Intranet** zone, then click the **Custom Level...** button.

6. Configure the required security options. Click **OK**.

7. Click **OK** to close the Internet Options.

8.5.6 CHANGE THE COOKIE LEVEL

Scenario

You use a Windows XP computer at home. You have a broadband connection to the Internet through your local cable provider, and use the computer mostly for surfing the web. However, you frequently receive messages about cookie handling not being enabled. You are not concerned about the security of your computer, because you have no sensitive information on it.

Configure the privacy setting for your computer to the Low default level.

Note: To open the Internet Options applet, use the Classic View in the Control Panel.

Steps

Complete the following steps:

1. Click **Start/Control Panel.**

2. Click **Switch to Classic View.**

3. Double-click **Internet Options.**

4. Click the **Privacy** tab. The following dialog is shown.

5. Move the slider to set the security level to **Low.** Click **OK.**

8.5.7 CUSTOMIZE COOKIE HANDLING

Scenario

You work on a Windows XP Professional computer. You are concerned about your privacy when surfing the web and would like to increase it. You want your computer to block cookies from banner ad companies such as Quadrupleclick.com, but you also want your computer to accept cookies from legitimate sites, such as your bank's web site.

Edit the privacy settings in Internet Options to implement the following cookie settings:

- Always allow 1st party cookies

- Always block 3rd party cookies

- Accept session cookies

Note: To open the Internet Options applet, use the Classic View in the Control Panel.

Steps

Complete the following steps:

1. Click **Start/Control Panel**.

2. Click **Switch to Classic View**.

3. Double-click **Internet Options**.

4. Click the **Privacy** tab.

5. Click the **Advanced...** button. The following dialog is shown.

6. Select **Override automatic cookie handling** and configure the desired cookie settings. Click **OK**.

7. Click **OK**.

8.5.8 CONFIGURE BROWSER SECURITY

Scenario

You are a computer programmer for your company. You often download code modules from various sites on the Internet to use in your own projects. Recently, you have been asked by your manager to proactively increase the security of your web surfing and downloading, so you decide to implement some advanced security measures in Internet Explorer.

Your tasks in this lab are to enable the following settings on your computer:

- Check for server certificate revocation

- Check for signatures on downloaded programs

Note: To open the Internet Options applet, use the Classic View in the Control Panel.

Steps

Complete the following steps:

1. Click **Start/Control Panel.**

2. Click **Switch to Classic View.**

3. Double-click **Internet Options.**

4. Click the **Advanced** tab. The following dialog is shown.

Internet Properties   ? X

| General | Security | Privacy | Content | Connections | Programs | Advanced |

Settings:

- 🔧 Accessibility
  - ☐ Always expand ALT text for images
  - ☐ Move system caret with focus/selection changes
- 🗔 Browsing
  - ☑ Always send URLs as UTF-8 (requires restart)
  - ☑ Automatically check for Internet Explorer updates
  - ☑ Closed unused folders in History and Favorites (requires restart)
  - ☑ Disable script debugging
  - ☐ Display a notification about every script error
  - ☑ Enable folder view for FTP sites
  - ☑ Enable Install On Demand (Internet Explorer)
  - ☑ Enable Install On Demand (Other)
  - ☑ Enable offline items to be synchronized on a schedule
  - ☑ Enable page transistions
  - ☐ Enable Personalized Favorites Menu
  - ☑ Enable third-party browser extensions (requires restart)
  - ☑ Enable visual styles on buttons and controls in web pages

[Restore Defaults]

[OK]   [Cancel]   [Apply]

By default, which SSL levels are enabled?

_____

By default, what action will take place when an invalid site certificate is received?

_____

5. Enable or disable the features you want to customize.

6. Click **OK**.

8.5.10 USE A PROXY SERVER

Scenario

You have just started night classes at SimUniversity, an online university. The university library is accessible from your computer through the Internet. However, because of licensing agreements, SimUniversity must control access to the library catalog. They use a proxy server to do this.

Your task in this lab is to configure the following proxy server settings:

- Edit the LAN Settings to automatically detect proxy settings.

- Configure the connection to use the following automatic configuration script when connecting:

    http:\\proxy.simuniversity.edu:9000/proxy.pac

Note: To open the Internet Options applet, use the Classic View in the Control Panel.

Steps

Complete the following steps:

1. Click **Start/Control Panel.**

2. Select **Switch to Classic View,** then double-click the **Internet Options** applet.

3. Select the **Connections** tab. The following dialog is shown.

4. Click the **LAN Settings...** button to open the following dialog.

5. Select the **Automatically detect settings** box.

What effect does this action have on the configuration options available to you?

_____

6. Select the **Use automatic configuration script** box.

How is the effect of selecting this option different from the previous option you selected?

_____

7. Enter the location of the script given in the scenario in the **Address** text box, then click **OK**.

9.0

System Management

9.2.4 ENABLE REMOTE DESKTOP

Scenario

To allow the Technicians to audit and configure user settings from their workstations, you want to enable Remote Desktop on the computers in your company.

Your task in this lab is to do the following:

- Enable Remote Desktop on the current machine.

- Add the following users to the access list:

  ○ Rodney Haddie (username = rhaddie)

  ○ Julie Niles (username = jniles)

- Allow Remote Desktop through the firewall.

Steps

You can enable the Remote Desktop setting through the System Properties dialog box.

Complete the following steps:

1. Click the **Start** button, then right-click **My Computer** and select **Properties**.

2. Select the **Remote** tab. The following dialog is shown.

3. Select the option that allows users to connect to the computer remotely, then click the **Select Remote Users...** button to add remote connection users. The following dialog is shown.

4. Click the **Add...** button.

5. Click the **Advanced...** button, then click **Find Now**.

6. Select the users whom you wish to add, then click **OK**.

7. Click **OK** until you exit the System Properties box.

8. With Remote Desktop enabled and users added, you must allow it to operate through the firewall. To do so, open the Control Panel by clicking **Start/Control Panel**.

9. Select **Switch to Classic View.**

10. Double-click the **Windows Firewall** applet. The following dialog opens.

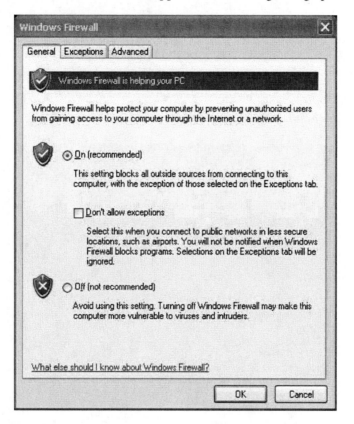

11. Click the **Exceptions** tab.

What types of traffic can you allow through the firewall?

_____

Notice that Remote Desktop traffic is allowed by default after you enable Remote Desktop.

12. Click **OK.**

9.3.4 CONFIGURE AUTOMATIC UPDATES

Scenario

You are configuring a new computer for a new employee. The update policy allows you to download and install updates automatically. Additionally, you want the system to find and update its drivers automatically.

Your task in this lab is to do the following:

- Configure updates to download and install each Wednesday at 2 AM.

- Allow the system to search for updated drivers automatically.

Steps

Complete the following steps:

1. Click **Start**, then right-click **My Computer** and select **Properties**.

2. Click the **Automatic Updates** tab. The following dialog is shown.

3. Select **Automatic (recommended)**, then configure the day and time.

4. To configure automatic driver updating, click the **Hardware** tab.

5. Click the **Windows Update** button to open a screen similar to the one you see here.

6. Select the option that automatically finds device drivers, then click **OK**.

7. Click **OK** to apply the changes.

9.4.4 CREATE A RESTORE POINT

Scenario

You are preparing to do an upgrade of a user's computer. Prior to performing the upgrade, you want to set a system restore point. Your task in this lab is to create a system restore point called *Restore Point 1*.

Steps

Use the System Restore Point wizard to create a restore point.

Complete the following steps:

1. Open the System Restore Point wizard by clicking **Start/All Programs/Accessories/ System Tools/System Restore**. The following screen is shown.

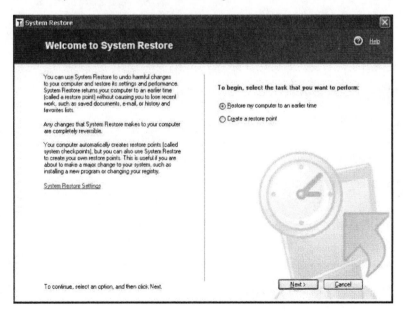

2. Select **Create a restore point,** then click **Next.** The following screen is shown.

3. Enter the description required by the scenario and click **Create.**

4. To view the restore point, click the **Home** button.

5. Select **Restore my computer to an earlier time,** then click **Next.**

   What is the date and time of the restore point you created?

   _____

6. Click **Cancel** to exit the wizard.

9.4.5 RESTORE TO A POINT IN TIME

Scenario

After running a software update, a user says that her computer locks up and won't respond. You want to restore the system to a point prior to the software update.

Your task in this lab is to restore the system using the **Restore Point 3** restore point created on 5/15/2006.

Steps

Use the System Restore Point wizard to restore the system to a previous state.

Complete the following steps:

1. Open the System Restore Point wizard by clicking **Start/All Programs/Accessories/System Tools/System Restore.**

2. Select the option that allows you to restore your computer to a previous state, then click **Next.** The following screen is shown.

3. In the calendar, select the date required by the scenario, then select the appropriate restore point. Click **Next**. The results should be similar to the screen you see here.

4. Click **Next**, then click **OK** when prompted to restart the computer. (**Note:** The lab does not allow you to reboot.)

5. Click **OK**.

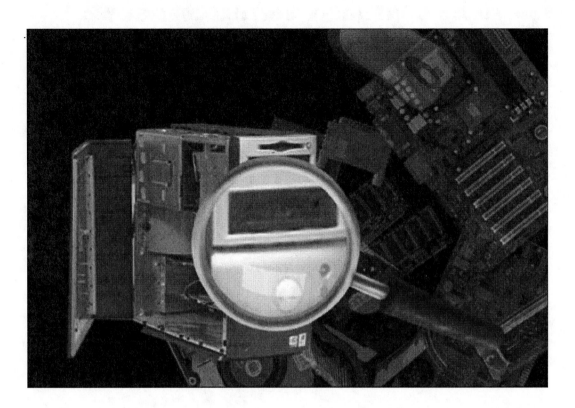

10.0
Troubleshooting

10.1.9 CONFIGURE VIRTUAL MEMORY

Scenario

You want to optimize performance by moving the swap file from the C: drive where the operating system files are to another drive.

Your task in this lab is to do the following:

- Delete the swap file on the C: drive.

- Create a swap file on the D: drive using the following specifications:

    ○ Initial size: 768 MB

    ○ Maximum size: 1536 MB

Steps

You can optimize the virtual memory performance by moving the paging file (swap file) from the hard disk where the operating system files reside.

Complete the following steps:

1. Click **Start,** then right-click **My Computer** and select **Properties.**

2. Select the **Advanced** tab.

3. Click the **Settings** button in the Performance section.

4. Click the **Advanced** tab. The following dialog is shown.

5. Click the **Change** button to edit the virtual memory configuration. The following dialog is shown.

6. Make sure **C:** is selected, then select **No paging file**. Click the **Set** button.

7. Select the **D:** drive, then choose the **Custom size** option and set the initial and new sizes. Click **Set**.

8. Click **OK**.

10.4.4 CONFIGURE WINDOWS REPORTING

Scenario

You do not want to report errors to Microsoft, but you do want to know if your system encounters a critical error. Your task in this lab is to disable Windows reporting, but have critical errors reported to you.

Steps

Complete the following steps:

1. Click the **Start** button, then right-click **My Computer** and select **Properties**.

2. Select the **Advanced** tab. The following dialog is shown.

3.   Click the **Error Reporting** button. The following dialog is shown.

4.   Configure error reporting to occur according to the scenario requirements.

5.   Click **OK** to save the changes and exit.

10.5.4 ROLL BACK A DRIVER

Scenario

The manufacturer of your video card released an updated driver. You downloaded and installed the driver, but now you cannot replay video on your machine. You want to roll back the driver for the video adapter to the previous driver.

Steps

Complete the following steps:

1. Click the **Start** button, then right-click **My Computer** and select **Manage**.

2. Select **Device Manager** in the left pane.

3. Expand the **Display adapters** node.

4. Double-click the **32MB NVDIA GeForce2 MX with TV Out** device.

5. Select the **Driver** tab to view a page similar to the one shown here.

6. Click the **Roll Back Driver** button.

7. Click **Yes** to confirm the rollback operation.

8. Click **OK** to exit the driver properties box, then click **OK** again to restart your computer.